PRAISE FOR *RECLAIMING OUR FORGOTTEN HERITAGE*

"This book will warm your heart and invite you on a journey to reclaiming your own heritage in Christ and cause you to remember who you are, because you are renewing your mind to know who the Triune God truly is!"

—Dr. Mark J. Chironna, Church On The Living Edge,
Mark Chironna Ministries, Longwood, Florida

"This very compelling message punctuates the big-picture as well as the personal restoration underway today, globally and in Israel, that is releasing God's people into their true identity, purpose, and destiny."

—Morris Ruddick, Christian author and speaker,
entrepreneur and consultant to Fortune 500
companies, economic community development missionary

"Many Christians probably wonder why they love Israel so intensely and why they are so defensive of her people and the land. It is simply because we came from the same umbilical cord. Curt Landry has masterfully used his craft as a wordsmith to reattach us to our Hebraic roots."

—John A. Kilpatrick, founder and senior pastor,
Church of His Presence, Daphne, Alabama

"By inviting us to examine our forgotten spiritual inheritance, Rabbi Curt Landry takes us closer to the 'many mansions' on the horizon. Delve deeply into the passages; expect to meet love and experience liberty."

—Evangelist Alveda King

"Outstanding, a must-read for every Christian! Curt Landry has utilized his unique ability to inform and inspire. A one-of-a-kind book for your library."

—Pastor Happy Caldwell

Reclaiming Our

FORGOTTEN
HERITAGE

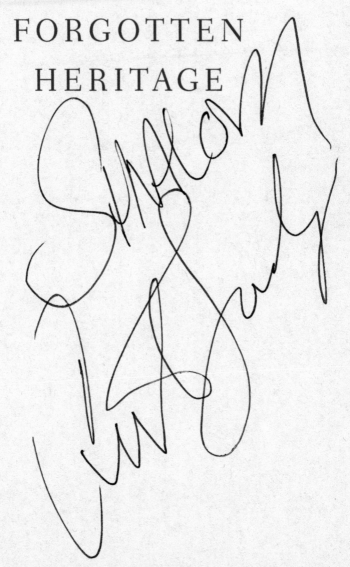

Reclaiming Our
FORGOTTEN
HERITAGE

HOW UNDERSTANDING THE
JEWISH ROOTS *of* CHRISTIANITY
CAN TRANSFORM
YOUR FAITH

CURT LANDRY

NELSON
BOOKS
An Imprint of Thomas Nelson

Published in Nashville, Tennessee, by Nelson Books, an imprint of Thomas Nelson. Nelson Books and Thomas Nelson are registered trademarks of HarperCollins Christian Publishing, Inc.

Author is represented by the literary agency of The Fedd Agency, Inc., P. O. Box 341973, Austin, Texas 78734.

Thomas Nelson titles may be purchased in bulk for educational, business, fund-raising, or sales promotional use. For information, please e-mail SpecialMarkets@ThomasNelson.com.

Unless otherwise noted, Scripture quotations are taken from the New King James Version®. © 1982 by Thomas Nelson. Used by permission. All rights reserved.

Scripture quotations marked ESV are from the ESV® Bible (The Holy Bible, English Standard Version®). Copyright © 2001 by Crossway, a publishing ministry of Good News Publishers. Used by permission. All rights reserved.

Scripture quotations marked KJV are from the King James Version. Public domain.

Scripture quotations marked NIV are from the Holy Bible, New International Version®, NIV®. Copyright © 1973, 1978, 1984, 2011 by Biblica, Inc.® Used by permission of Zondervan. All rights reserved worldwide. www.Zondervan.com. The "NIV" and "New International Version" are trademarks registered in the United States Patent and Trademark Office by Biblica, Inc.®

Scripture quotations marked NLT are from the Holy Bible, New Living Translation. © 1996, 2004, 2007, 2013, 2015 by Tyndale House Foundation. Used by permission of Tyndale House Publishers, Inc., Carol Stream, Illinois 60188. All rights reserved.

Emphasis in Scripture has been added by the author.

ISBN 978-1-4002-0946-0 (eBook)
ISBN 978-1-4002-0940-8 (TP)

Library of Congress Control Number: 2018948945

Printed in the United States of America

19 20 21 22 23 LSC 10 9 8 7 6 5 4 3 2 1

This book is dedicated to my family: my wife Christie, whose prayers brought me salvation, and to my daughter Megann, my son-in-law Paul, and my granddaughter Ariebella.

And to our ministry family at House of David.

This book is not just my story; it is our story.

CONTENTS

FOREWORD

CURT LANDRY AND I SHARE a love for the nation of Israel and the Jewish roots of the Christian faith. We have been friends and worked together since 2009 as we both not only value our shared spiritual heritage but also the prophetic nature of God. In 2009 Voice of Evangelism partnered with Curt's organization My Olive Tree to adopt a large olive grove in the Galilee region of Israel. We did so in order to help preserve the precious olive trees during a severe drought, provide work for Jewish people in Israel, and use oil from the grove to produce special anointing oil based upon the biblical patterns found in Exodus. This anointing oil has since gone around the world and anointed the nations out of Zion.

Interestingly enough this project was met with some opposition and it has been clear that many do not understand the priesthood, our identity in the priesthood, or the roots of our Christian faith. They questioned our "right" to make anointing oil according to biblical instruction—something you would not question if you understood our heritage. Through this process we can see many in the church robbed of covenant blessings based on misunderstanding and misinterpretation of the scripture (Exodus 30:25).

In the New Testament we are told that if a believer is sick, we are to "anoint them with oil in the name of the Lord" (James

5:14–15 NIV). However, in biblical times the oil was strictly reserved for use by the priests. But notice what the Bible teaches about believers in Revelation 1:6, saying: "And hath made us kings and priests unto God and his Father; to him be glory and dominion for ever and ever" (KJV). The Greek can read a "kingdom of priests."

He has made *us*. This is *our identity*.

Under the old covenant no common person could slay a sacrifice, sprinkle blood on the altar, and enter the holy place to offer incense, light the menorah, or be anointed with the oil. However, as a kingdom of priests we now offer our sacrifices of praise and it is our spiritual position as priests unto God that enables believers to use anointing oil for the purpose of anointing a person!

Without an understanding of biblical covenant and the roots of our heritage these mysteries would have remained veiled—but through this revelation God has brought restitution and great blessing.

Curt and I continue to co-labor together on this project as well as adopt olive trees in Israel to put our faith in action and to leave a legacy of truth for our children and our grandchildren. We are *reclaiming our forgotten heritage* not only in word but also in deed working together as the "One New Man"—a concept that Curt Landry explains in-depth in the upcoming chapters.

Curt Landry's *Reclaiming Our Forgotten Heritage* serves as a timely and groundbreaking take on the roots of the Christian church and its place in the entirety of God's kingdom. As Landry uncovers and unwraps the discovery of his own Jewish heritage and history, he also seeks to do the same for the body of Christ. This book attempts to answer the questions "Who are we?" and "Why are we here?" from the perspective of the whole body of believers. If we ignore some of the full story, we are missing some part of our identity—and in identity there is power, there is purpose, and there is covenant.

Reclaiming Our Forgotten Heritage provides a valuable and unique take on this situation. As the body of Christ begins to reconnect with the olive tree onto which it has been grafted and as the fulfillment of Revelation draws nearer, there is no better time than now to learn about and become firmly grounded within your spiritual heritage.

Perry Stone, founder, Voice of
Evangelism, International School
of the Word, Omega Center
International, and Manna Fest

INTRODUCTION

> *Therefore remember that you, once Gentiles in the*
> *flesh—who are called Uncircumcision by what is called*
> *the Circumcision made in the flesh by hands—that at*
> *that time you were without Christ, being aliens from the*
> *commonwealth of Israel and strangers from the covenants*
> *of promise, having no hope and without God in the world.*
> *But now in Christ Jesus you who once were far off have*
> *been brought near by the blood of Christ.*
>
> —EPHESIANS 2:11–13

THE TWENTY-FIRST-CENTURY CHURCH is in the midst of an identity crisis.

The problem is we worship a Jesus we've never gotten to know for who He fully is, and because of that, we don't know who we are when we come to the Father. As a result, we don't have the influence or affluence God intended His church to have. Secular culture is steamrolling us, not because the world is growing darker and the return of Christ is imminent (though it is), but because we're out of alignment with the true biblical roots of our faith. While that isn't enough to deprive us of God's grace, it is enough to separate us from the blessings of being aligned with an open heaven, a place where you can experience open communication with God and the Spirit moves freely. This is causing us to miss out on the fullness of our Christian heritage, and I believe it is a big part of why Christian values are losing their voice in the affairs of our nations today.

I know what it's like to wonder about your identity. I was born an orphan, rejected by my biological family on both sides, and despite having wonderful, loving adoptive parents and siblings, I knew nothing of my biological heritage for more than thirty-five years.

If you would have asked me when I was growing up or even in my twenties and early thirties if I had a void in my identity, I would have told you no. I thought I was fine. But there was still something missing, and at some level I felt it. The identity I had created for myself was not the identity God intended for me to have. I had no real understanding of where I came from or who my father was. So I ended up searching for identity and purpose in many different places and ended up a counterfeit of what God wanted me to be. I am so thankful He awoke me to the truth.

Despite often being the heroes of fairy tales, orphans have neither heritage nor roots. That's what makes them so vulnerable and so easily taken advantage of. Almost every such tale, in fact, is the story of an orphaned child coming of age to discover his or her heritage and royal identity. Think of Cinderella, Snow White, King Arthur, Pinocchio, the beast in *Beauty and the Beast*, or that ugly duckling—each one essentially involved in a quest for true identity.

Without a family heritage to look back on, orphans and adoptees alike tend to be culturally adrift. Loving adoptive parents can compensate for this quite a bit, but that deep-down longing to know who we are and where we came from persists. In fact, even those who grew up in the family they were born into may find themselves wondering about their ancestry.

I think that's a big part of why genealogy kits are so popular today. We've so mixed our cultures and backgrounds, and people are hungry to know their ancestral and ethnic histories. They figure the best way to find that out is to uncover their roots and heritage as it has been recorded in their DNA. It's all part of how we answer the universal questions of "Who am I?" and "Why am I here?"

Those questions persist in today's church as well. We are living in what many call a "post-Christian" era, which means that many come into church fellowship as spiritual orphans, trying to find their place in the family of God but disconnected from previous generations. Some of their insights into the Scriptures are refreshing, but they struggle to find footing in those Scriptures because they're reading them completely disconnected from their true foundation.

No wonder so many are wandering off onto theological thin ice. No wonder so many churches are anemic and seem to be crumbling. In biblical terms, they've built their houses on the sand, without firm foundations. Our biblical heritage has been hijacked and replaced with a counterfeit identity and disconnected traditions. We call ourselves Christian, but the full meaning of that term has been lost because we've become separated from the truth of God's complete story in His pursuit of humanity. Because of this, our faith is like a tree with shallow roots. Rituals have lost their meaning; we don't know why we do what we do or how to find our way back to the fullness of who we are in Christ.

But I've got good news. All is not lost. God is reviving His church and reinvigorating His kingdom family. How? By reconnecting us to our historic roots so we can reclaim our forgotten heritage.

When I was thirty-eight years old, newly born again and quite content to be a Landry (the name of my adoptive family), God told me to reach out and reconnect with my biological father. *What?* was my first thought. *Why?* was my second.

I had never been very curious about my biological parents nor wondered much about why they'd given me up. Ray and Rita Landry *were* my mom and dad, and they often reminded me that I was special because I hadn't just been born into their family but they had chosen me. They were wonderful, loving people who raised me as their own. There was no dysfunctional family history that drove me to find my "real" parents.

God knew that, of course, and His reasons for having me reach out had nothing to do with the usual reasons most adopted kids want to find their biological parents. Instead, God wanted to connect me with a lost heritage that, over the next twenty-plus years, has changed my life and my influence forever. It's fueled my purpose and helped me understand why I'm here on the earth for such a time as this. It has given me a mission, provided me with a means to touch tens of thousands of lives, and connected me with a message that I believe can do the same for you.

That day when I spoke with my biological father, he told me something I would never have guessed, even though it had been hinted at all my life. I found out that day that my biological mother was Jewish. Suddenly so many things started to make sense. I'd had so many connections with Jewish people over the years, and several people assumed I was Jewish. I was given back a heritage that being given up for adoption had stolen away.

It was a gift that has taken me more than twenty years to unwrap.

You see, when I started to reconnect with my personal Jewish roots in the interest of finding out more about my identity, a remarkable thing happened along the way: I learned things about my identity in Christ that few other Christians seemed to have any clue about. As I learned about the Jewish faith and traditions, I began to read the New Testament Scriptures with a greater depth of understanding. And when I traveled to Israel, I began to make connections I would have never made otherwise. I've made more than forty trips there now and learned so much from the Israeli mind-set. Discovering my heritage brought a new fullness to my life and to my faith.

As it turned out, connecting with my "real" father taught me more about connecting with my heavenly Father than I had ever imagined possible. I already loved Jesus and had accepted Him as my Lord and Savior, but it's only been in exploring and understanding my Jewish roots that I've come to understand the full significance of that reality. Those revelations about my identity have infused my life with purpose and meaning.

If you are a Christian—if you are, as Paul described it in Romans 11, a wild olive branch grafted into the cultivated olive tree that is Israel—then that same heritage and blessing are available to you. You, too, can be part of "the chosen people of God" if you will only strive to understand and step into it as I have learned to do.

Please don't misunderstand me. I'm not suggesting we need to return to the Hebrew law in some legalistic sense. Christ fulfilled the law. Jesus' sacrifice on the cross was enough for now and forevermore. His work is complete. When He said, "It is finished," He spoke the truth. What He'd come to accomplish was done, and the new covenant was ratified and irrevocably sealed through His shed blood. We are saved by faith, not by works. It is by being born again of the Spirit of God that we "enter the kingdom of God" (John 3:5).

But who wants to just slide in and hang around the gates our whole Christian lives? There are so many riches to be discovered if we venture further in.

To realize the fullness of Christ's kingdom—to become His bride, the church, spotless and without blemish, eternal and triumphant and ready for His return—we need to understand the fullness of the two testaments and the promises therein. We need to believe He is eager to fulfill the prayer He gave us in Matthew 6:10:

> Your kingdom come.
> Your will be done
> on earth as it is in heaven.

We need a deeper understanding of Jesus as the Messiah promised to the Hebrews, of what God has been doing by restoring Israel in 1948 to the land He promised them so many centuries before, and of the power to be found in standing with Israel not only as political allies but as joint heirs in a spiritual inheritance that we will not receive without them—and that they will not receive without us.

To help you understand this forgotten heritage that God has been holding in waiting for us, I want to invite you into my story, a story God has taught me strangely parallels that of His church. Just as I, born Jewish, was adopted into a Gentile family and disconnected from my heritage, so, too, the church, originally Jewish, got disconnected from her heritage when Rome took her over under Constantine, cutting her off from her Hebraic origins and interpreting her tenets and teachings through the lens of Hellenized philosophy (Greek culture, influence, and religion that extended beyond the nation of Greece and into foreign lands either conquered by Greece or greatly influenced by her dominance). But in the same way I learned of my true heritage and have reconnected with it, I believe God is reconnecting His church with her Hebraic beginnings today. In the process, He is reinfusing her with identity, purpose, and power so that she will be ready as the bride He will return for.

Again, I'm not saying this is a return to the law as a means of justifying our faith—Paul was quite clear on that in the book of Romans and elsewhere. But I believe the Romans threw the baby out with the bathwater when they disconnected Christianity from its Jewish origins. We've lost the fullness of the Christian experience and much of the meaning of why God decided to save the world through the house of David and a Jewish boy named Yeshua.[1]

My heart's desire is that my personal testimony of reclaiming my forgotten heritage—both physically and spiritually—will become a source of encouragement and a road map that you can follow to discover your own purpose, destiny, and identity. I truly believe that as you uncover the lost roots of your spiritual heritage and engage with the key elements of covenant alignment, you can live more fully and leave a powerful legacy.

Christ isn't planning to come back to an impotent, traumatized, defeated bride. He wants to mature the church to the fullness of grace and stature first. He wants us as Christians to step into the destinies He set for each of us before the foundations of the world. But to realize these things, we need to understand His original intents and unveil the mysteries and manifold wisdom of His plans to the universe. We need to understand the fullness of the two testaments and the meanings, stipulations, and promises of His covenants. They define us as believers. They give us a place to stand, and they give us a lever with which to move the earth.

I believe God is calling us back to our heritage so that He can show us our true identities as believers and followers of Jesus Christ. That has been the journey of my life, and I believe it is a story that can help you find your unique identity, purpose, and power in Him.

one

—

THE POWER OF
HERITAGE

> *Therefore whoever hears these sayings of Mine, and*
> *does them, I will liken him to a wise man who built his*
> *house on the rock: and the rain descended, the floods*
> *came, and the winds blew and beat on that house; and*
> *it did not fall, for it was founded on the rock.*
>
> —MATTHEW 7:24–25

GOD'S DESIGN WAS NEVER THAT we would come into the world to be alone.

From the moment of our birth, we start reaching out for others in a world that is totally alien and unintelligible to us. We first learn to focus, see, and understand our world by gazing into the loving eyes of our mothers as we nurse. The first thing we recognize is her face. Before we know anything about the world around us, we know who our parents are and find comfort in their loving embrace. God designed the nuclear family as a place of protection and foundation. As we learn about the world around us, God intended that we do that hand in hand with our moms and dads.

In fact, the Bible instructs:

> Now this is the commandment, and these are the statutes and judgments which the LORD your God has commanded to teach you, that you may observe them in the land which you are crossing over to possess, that you may fear the LORD your God, to keep all His statutes and His commandments which I command you, *you and your son and your grandson*, all the days of your life, and that your days may be prolonged. . . .
>
> And these words which I command you today shall be in your heart. You shall teach them diligently to your children, and shall talk of them when you sit in your house, when you walk by the way, when you lie down, and when you rise up. You shall bind them as a sign on your hand, and they shall be as frontlets between your eyes. You shall write them on the doorposts of your house and on your gates. (Deuteronomy 6:1–2, 6–9, emphasis added)

In this passage, God wasn't just talking about educating our children. He was talking about creating a heritage of faith, of grounding our children in the wisdom of God and helping form their identities as God's creation here on the earth, intended to take dominion of it and prosper it. It's not just head learning, and it's more than just heart learning; it's digging deep to expose the foundation of who our children are as members of our families stretching back through generations, as citizens of a nation and as ambassadors of the kingdom of God. It is raising them the way Solomon counseled in Proverbs 22:6:

> Train up a child in the way he should go,
> And when he is old he will not depart from it.

Why won't they depart from it? Because their awareness has been saturated in their heritage, their foundation, and their identity.

When we raise up our children in this way, they don't see themselves as free agents disconnected from any responsibility or purpose in the world around them. They learn they're not here only to "have fun" and to "find happiness." They have entered life as part of a tradition founded on contributing to the world around them, with responsibilities to every human being they encounter. They've been instilled with values built on wisdom greater than the insights of their own tiny brains, but they've also brought something of their own to contribute to it. They are part of a tribe that is here to do the will of God, but they also have their own individual mark to make.

I know how countercultural that can sound to Americans and those of Western society today. We've long been fiercely independent and have guarded our individual rights as sacred, taking to heart what Thomas Jefferson wrote in the Declaration of Independence:

> We hold these truths to be self-evident, that all men are cre-
> ated equal, that they are endowed by their Creator with certain
> unalienable Rights, that among these are Life, Liberty and the
> pursuit of Happiness.[1]

And great good has come from these values, but I believe the pendulum has swung so far toward the individual that we are in danger of losing the wisdom of our collective past. Kids are encouraged to go out and find their own ways with only minimal understanding of their heritage and little formation in their faith. I've spoken with parents who are actually afraid to talk about values and traditions with their children for fear they may prejudice them in some way from finding "their own truth."

No wonder we have a generation today that is coming into adulthood with "orphaned" spirits. No wonder they're hungry for their roots and fascinated with stories of heritage. Look at the popularity of television shows like *Downton Abbey* and *The Crown* and of magazines and websites featuring stories and pictures of monarchs and their heirs. The idea of nobility and royalty—of the passing down of a heritage that means something and brings privilege with it—fascinates people worldwide. We're hungry to have a place to stand, to know where we belong in the world with respect to everyone else, to be significant in some way, to make a difference for having existed. It's why we long to make our mark and to find meaning in our lives.

But rather than growing up with that and launching into life with a foundational sense of who we are and the difference we are here to make, so many who enter adulthood today haven't even begun that journey. You don't have to look far to see it. Look at the average freshman college dorm today. The rites of passage that take place in those halls have nothing to do with our culture or heritage, or upholding any sense of traditional values, but instead with determining how much alcohol someone can consume and still walk, experimenting sexually, and "trying to find themselves." They are launched into a perpetual adolescence that often doesn't end until their forties. And we're doing them a great disservice by letting them flounder like this.

But the same isn't true of all young people and cultures, and there's a great deal we can learn from these counterexamples.

I recently met a young woman in Israel who astounded me. She'd been raised Jewish in England but had become an Israeli citizen. She had served in the Israeli army and was putting in seventy-plus hours a week running her own nonprofit, even though her parents provided her with enough money that she would never need to work a day in her life.

Our first meeting, which had been set up by one of the wealthiest Jewish men in the world, took place at her company offices in Tel Aviv. She arrived a little late, so my son-in-law, Paul, and I were already there. She emerged from her limousine wearing Birkenstocks, jeans, and a T-shirt. Despite being dressed like some hipster barista in the United States, she had an air of confidence and conviction about her.

She apologized for being late, explaining that they'd run into a little more traffic than expected while dropping off her kids at their private school in Herzliya (a township north of Tel Aviv, along one of Israel's finest beaches). She spoke English with a British accent, but I would learn that she also spoke impeccable Hebrew. She invited Paul and me into her office, asked if we'd like a cup of tea or coffee, and offered us a seat.

It didn't take long to figure out she'd done her homework on me, and every word she spoke was respectful. She told me about the work she was doing in Israel. Her foundation brought in bloggers from around the world—anyone whose work had garnered more than a million hits in a day—so they could get to know her country. It didn't matter if their blogs were about food, tech, fashion, or whatever. Her organization sponsored their trip to Israel, where they spent a week to ten days speaking to their Israeli counterparts about what they did and learning about what the Israelis were doing. The expectation was that they'd go back home and blog about their visit: "Hey, listen. I'm from Berlin. I was told this about Israel, but I just spent ten days there, and this is what I did, and this is what I learned."

I thought the idea was brilliant. I thought *she* was brilliant.

Not only did Israelis learn from each visitor, but each visitor went home as a champion of Israel. But I had to ask, "Why do you do all of this? Why do you work so hard? I know your family. You don't have to work."

She told me, "I must work because I'm not in the army anymore. My war now is in our economy. We know that if we don't keep the economy strong in Israel, our neighbors will overtake us, so our economic health and development is just as important as our air force and our army. So I work to be able to strengthen our country so that my children will have a place to live. As Jews, as you know, if we don't have Israel, there will be no place for us to live as a people."

It seemed so crazy. Here was a young woman worth millions, living in a beautiful house on the beach. She shouldn't have had a care in the world. But she was working seventy-plus hours a week to keep the economy of her country strong *so that her children would have a place to live when they grew up.* She seemed like a kid to me, though she was probably in her thirties, and she was living with purpose in a way I didn't learn about until I was in my fifties.

And yet I meet people with a similar drive every time I visit Israel. In that tiny little country, they seem to be everywhere. It's as if it's in the air they breathe.

My experience is very different in the United States. Outside of our daughter, Megann, and her husband, Paul, whom I see almost every day, I very rarely meet young people like that young woman in Tel Aviv.

Why? The only reason I can think of is their sense of heritage—or lack of it.

Heritage is primarily passed down through traditional activities, values, and holidays. Whether we understand it or not, the way we use our time, mark our calendars, and celebrate our culture provides a constant, subliminal reminder of who we are, where we came from, and what we believe is important to maintain. These activities and traditions and customs, big and small—you could call them "memorial activities"—keep us tied to the foundation of our past, both the good and the bad. They become like patterns in our souls, like predictable tides, so that we instinctively honor those who have gone before us, what they experienced and persevered through, and what wisdom and learning they passed on.

Most families, for example, always eat certain foods at Thanksgiving. We enjoy these dishes, of course, not only because they are delicious but also because they remind us of who we are and where we came from. They are prepared with love and in memory of the family member who first made them. Eating them tends to evoke familiar family stories and the sharing of memories. Such traditions help strengthen us in who we aspire to become and remind us of positive life lessons learned from our shared experiences together and from past generations.

At our church, House of David, we often say, "Our ceiling should become our children's floor." The nature of heritage is leaving a legacy of truth and experience so that our children and grandchildren can learn from us and do not have to make the same mistakes we did. Our children should be able to grow in strength and wisdom because of the gifts of this family legacy.

Some cultures are very good at doing that. Over the centuries, for example, the Jewish people have become masters at handing down a heritage of wisdom and identity. You don't have to dig too deeply to see this. It manifests itself in many ways. Just for the sake of comparison, however, I want to focus on the area of material success—yes, money.

Please understand, I'm not saying that money is everything. It's not. I'm certainly not trying to reinforce the "rich Jewish" stereotype that has led to such distortion and even persecution over the years. I just want to use this one example to explore how different viewpoints, garnered from different heritages, can manifest different results in people's lives. And in general, the Jewish heritage seems to include a tremendous, understated work ethic that yields results, including financial ones.

Economic statistics certainly seem to bear this observation out. While the percentage of Jews in the United States is somewhere between 1.7 and 2.6 percent, 20 percent of the top fifty billionaires in the United States are Jewish.[2] And Pew Research has found that American Jewish households are significantly better off financially than any other group, with 44 percent having an annual income of one hundred thousand dollars or more and only 16 percent (the smallest percentage) making less than thirty thousand. (Even the wealthiest Christian group, Episcopalians, have significantly fewer people in the top bracket at 36 percent, while their group at the bottom is slightly larger at 17 percent.) Sadly, when you look at more Evangelical denominations like the Assemblies of God, their highest tiers of earners are much, much smaller at 10 percent, and the lower tier represents nearly half their members.[3]

Why the difference? Knowing a number of Jews and Christians in these different groups, the only thing I can put my finger on is that the Jews grew up with significantly different beliefs about money.

Jewish people—again, in general—tend to see money as a tool to accomplish tasks and feel it is part of their spiritual heritage to prosper. They feel it is important to prosper materially so they can be generous and accomplish their aspirations. With very few exceptions, there are no vows of poverty in Judaism, nor do very many Jews consider it intrinsically spiritual to be poor. How can you be a blessing to others if you don't have a surplus to give?

In addition, the Jewish scriptural tradition—from the same

Household income of U.S. religious groups
% of each religious group with total family income of____per year

	<$30,000	$30,000-49,999	$50,000-99,999	$100,000+
Jewish	16%	15%	24%	44%
Hindu	17	13	34	36
Episcopal Church	19	13	34	35
Presbyterian Church (U.S.A.)	24	15	29	32
Atheist	24	18	28	30
Agnostic	22	18	30	29
Orthodox Christian	18	17	36	29
United Church of Christ	31	16	23	29
Evangelical Lutheran Church in America	19	22	32	26
United Methodist Church	23	20	31	26
Presbyterian Church in America	27	17	31	25
Unitarian Universalist	30	17	30	23
Lutheran Church-Missouri Synod	22	21	34	22
Mormon	27	20	33	20
Muslim	34	17	29	20
All U.S. adults	35	20	26	19
Catholic	36	19	26	19
"Nothing in particular"	38	21	24	17
Churches of Christ	37	23	24	16
Southern Baptist Convention	32	22	31	16
Seventh-day Adventist	37	24	24	15
Buddhist	36	18	32	13
Assemblies of God	43	23	24	10
American Baptist Churches USA	53	18	21	9
Church of God in Christ	46	26	19	9
National Baptist Convention	49	21	21	9
Jehovah's Witness	48	25	22	4

Note: Results recalculated to exclude nonresponse. Figures may not add to 100% due to rounding.
Source: 2014 U.S. Religious Landscape Study, conducted June 4-Sept. 30, 2014
PEW RESEARCH CENTER

Scriptures that are in the Old Testament of every Christian Bible—tells them that if they obey God and act according to His wisdom, wealth will certainly follow. Look at these verses, for instance:

> And you shall remember the LORD your God, for it is He who gives you power to get wealth, that He may establish His covenant which He swore to your fathers, as it is this day. (Deuteronomy 8:18)

> Honor the LORD with your possessions,
> And with the firstfruits of all your increase;
> So your barns will be filled with plenty,
> And your vats will overflow with new wine.
>
> (PROVERBS 3:9–10)

Note, however, that greed is not a Jewish value, nor is taking advantage of the poor. In fact, the very opposite is true. The Hebrew Scriptures repeatedly link both obedience and prosperity with care for the less fortunate. As Proverbs 19:17 advises,

> He who has pity on the poor lends to the LORD,
> And He will pay back what he has given.

Widows and orphans are to be given special consideration. The poor and the foreigner are to be given ways to provide for themselves. The edges of fields are to be left unharvested so that others can glean from them and have food to eat. (Look at the Bible story of Ruth as an example.) There are laws against charging other Jews interest for loans and others mandating regular times of debt forgiveness. And the purpose of all these practices, as mandated in Scripture, is that "there may be no poor among you; for the LORD will greatly bless you in the land which

the LORD your God is giving you to possess as an inheritance"
(Deuteronomy 15:4).

At first glance, this may appear to be exactly the opposite of
Jesus' oft-quoted words: "For you have the poor with you always"
(Matthew 26:11). I believe, however, that He meant something
quite different from what we usually understand His words to
mean. He was saying that the poor are always around when we
don't follow God's wisdom for caring for them.

Jews understand the principle of being a good steward over
what God has entrusted to us and do not consider financial blessing in itself either shameful or ill-gotten. To them, money is just
a tool like a hammer or knife—that can be used to do good or
harm depending on how it is wielded. They believe we must do
our best to be sure our hearts are right and then to wield whatever
resources we have for good.

As I see it, this aspect of the Jewish heritage—their view of
material wealth—differs dramatically from the views and assumptions of many in our Western culture, including many of my fellow
Christians. Many of us, in fact, have come to view money and
wealth as a spiritual force with an almost demonic nature. We've
succumbed to a kind of gnosticism, an ancient heresy that insists
all physical things are evil and only spiritual things are pure. In
this light Christianity and segments of American culture, either
consciously or subconsciously, have come to view wealth as evil in
and of itself. That doesn't mean we don't want wealth or seek after
it. We just harbor queasy feelings that it's wrong to do so, and as a
result our relationship with money may become warped by guilt,
denial, and envy.

Just look at the protests and accusations during the past
decade against the so-called One Percent (the very wealthiest
Americans), for example. Popularized by the Occupy Wall Street
Movement in 2011, the term epitomizes the attitude that material

prosperity is inherently bad. Many Americans seem to have acqui-
esced to the attitude that attaining wealth automatically means
taking advantage of someone else and that attaining prosperity is
inherently selfish, irresponsible, and immoral.

Ironically, most of us who live in the United States are already
among the top 1 percent on the planet when it comes to wealth.
According to the Global Rich List, a website that focuses on
global income inequality, anyone who makes more than $32,400
a year is in the top 1 percent of wage earners worldwide.[4] That,
of course, would include many of those who protest most vocally
against the One Percent.

Christians who hold this attitude also may assume that truly
spiritual people don't need to think about money because God
will provide. (The Jewish tradition would affirm that yes, God does
provide, but a big part of that provision is through the wisdom provided in His Word for handling money.) Then they preach and act
as if anyone who believes differently has a shallow, weak faith. To
them the truly holy take vows of poverty, and all rich people are
to be mistrusted and looked on with suspicion. How could one
who felt that way, even subconsciously, ever feel comfortable with
acquiring wealth, even for the purposes of sharing it?

Now, we don't usually blatantly state these beliefs. We may
not even be aware that we believe them. But they are elements
of a prevalent religious mind-set we may have absorbed without
consideration. I know I unconsciously accepted them myself as I
was growing up, and I needed to change my attitudes and thinking significantly as I came to understand the full truth of God's
Word on the matter. Had I not been able to do this, I would not
have been able to be a conduit for tens of millions of dollars in
charitable giving.

Again, this is just one example of how heritage affects attitudes and in turn affects a culture. There are many others. The

point is that somehow, often in a culture that is very different around them, Jews have had a way of holding to their values and heritage, and we see this reflected in the area of finance. In contrast, all too often, we Christians end up looking just like the culture around us, even though we say we value very different things. The point is this: what we believe or value manifests in our lives and creates a heritage. Drug and alcohol abuse, divorce, domestic violence, even chronic loneliness and depression all seem to be at similar levels within the church as among those who don't believe or don't attend.

We're even divided on the purpose and value of church. In a recent study, the Barna Group found:

> Adults who believe church is very important cite two reasons above the rest: to be closer to God (44%) and to learn about God (27%). One in five (22%) say they go to church because the Bible teaches fellowship with other believers [is important]. And in spite of a growing epidemic of loneliness, just one in ten report going to church because they are looking for community.[5]

Despite the fact that seeking to be closer to God is the number-one reason people say they go to church, a sense of such closeness is rare. Fewer than one in five of those interviewed stated they feel closer to God at church, even on a monthly basis. While the second most popular answer was that they attend to learn about God, only 6 percent of those polled said they learned something new about God or Jesus the last time they attended. Nearly two-thirds (61 percent) went on to say they hadn't gained any significant or new insights into their faith the last time they went either. While people appear aware that they have real spiritual needs, they don't seem to be finding any answers by attending church. As a result, many are "turning elsewhere."[6]

These are signs of identity crisis. These are signs that becoming a Christian today is having little transformative effect on the lives we lead. Why? *Because a branch cut off from its roots will bear no fruit.* And what are our roots as Christians? They are Jewish. The Jewish heritage, as encapsulated in what we call our Old Testament as well as in Yeshua and His disciples, is our heritage as well, and embracing it is crucial to living in our true identity as God's people.

God chose Abraham to be the first Jew because He knew Abraham would be a good father. God knew Abraham would create a family that would live differently from those around them, one that would live for God and according to His ways. Abraham created a heritage of following God for his family that would outlast

- four hundred years of slavery in Egypt;
- the destruction of Jerusalem and being taken captive in Babylon;
- centuries of Roman occupation;
- being scattered over the earth (the Diaspora); and
- being exiled from their homeland for more than eighteen hundred years.

That same heritage was so strong that it even outlasted the Holocaust and then led to the reformation of a nation state in the same place Israel had been repeatedly exiled from. (No defeated and dispersed people group has ever replanted itself as a nation in its original location, let alone done so after nearly two millennia.)

There is a reason the Jews have survived as a people, unique among the nations of the earth. They've never let go of their heritage—which, again, is our heritage too.

I believe it is time for the church of Jesus Christ to return to that heritage, to rebuild her spiritual walls according to God's plan for restoration, with the power and dominion promised in God's covenant with His bride, the church. This recovery process starts with us as believers walking in a victorious identity as covenant daughters and sons and as spiritual kings and priests (Revelation 5:9–10).[7] God does not want to leave even one of us begging at the gate, defeated and powerless. He has another plan, but He can't get it to us if we refuse to walk in our born-again birthright as the vine grafted into both testaments of the Book.

Many of us have been reading the Word of God through a typical Hellenized filter and applying it to our lives as such, but there is so much more to discover when we begin to dig into our spiritual heritage as it is rooted in Judaism. Reading the Word with an understanding of the culture that shaped it, of both the men who wrote it and the men and women who heard it, and from the perspective of covenant as the one new family in Christ and seeing Jesus as our chief Rabbi as well as chief Priest truly enriches your faith and helps you discover your own identity, purpose, and power in the midst of the cultural confusion plaguing our times.

There is much to discover and uncover in the lost roots and the forgotten heritage of our faith. Let's get back to the Jesus of the Bible and the heritage He meant for us to have.

two

THE PLACE OF
IDENTITY

> *Therefore take up the whole armor of God, that you*
> *may be able to withstand in the evil day, and having*
> *done all, to stand. Stand therefore.*
>
> —EPHESIANS 6:13–14

"I SWEAR TO YOU, I do not know the man!"

Peter's eyes blazed, and the man recoiled, holding up his palms as if in surrender.

Then the rooster crowed for the second time. Jesus' words flooded back to him: "Before the rooster crows twice, you will deny Me three times" (Mark 14:72).

Peter buried his face in his hands and turned away from the crowd at the fire. "What have I done?"

It had only been a few hours since he had shared the Passover meal with Jesus, but so much had changed. Peter had been sure then that big things were soon to come. And big things had come—but nothing like what Peter expected.

Jesus had been arrested and was now on trial for His life. And Peter, though gripped with fear like the other disciples, hadn't been able to stay away. He couldn't be inside to hear what was going on, but he'd decided to stay close. What he hadn't expected was that he might be exposed for having been with Jesus—and perhaps arrested as well. And faced with that possibility, he'd let his fear get the better of him. Rather than quietly supporting Jesus from nearby, as he'd intended, Peter had denied Jesus three times—just as Jesus had foretold.

Peter was in the midst of an identity crisis. Though bold in his speech as always, he wasn't yet strong enough in his belief to bet his life on it. He didn't yet know who he was. He didn't yet know what he stood for. He was not yet Peter the apostle, but merely a confused disciple unsure of what really mattered.

And even after seeing Jesus raised from the dead and encountering Him twice, Peter was still confused. When Jesus went to look for Peter again, where did He find him? Back at the job he'd had before Jesus called him to become a disciple. Peter was fishing. He must have thought something like, "Well, that was fun. I've never seen a man raised from the dead before. God is certainly wonderful and powerful. But now that Jesus is gone, I'd better get back to work."

But Jesus wasn't done with him yet. He still had more to teach Peter about who He really was.

The day He found Peter and a few other disciples, Jesus called them to the shore and had breakfast with them. Then, as John recounted it, He had a little conversation with His mixed-up disciple:

So when they had eaten breakfast, Jesus said to Simon Peter, "Simon, son of Jonah, do you love Me more than these?"

He said to Him, "Yes, Lord; You know that I love You."

He said to him, "Feed My lambs."

He said to him again a second time, "Simon, son of Jonah, do you love Me?"

He said to Him, "Yes, Lord; You know that I love You."

He said to him, "Tend My sheep."

He said to him the third time, "Simon, son of Jonah, do you love Me?" Peter was grieved because He said to him the third time, "Do you love Me?"

And he said to Him, "Lord, You know all things; You know that I love You."

Jesus said to him, "Feed My sheep. Most assuredly, I say to you, when you were younger, you girded yourself and walked where you wished; but when you are old, you will stretch out your hands, and another will gird you and carry you where you do not wish." This He spoke, signifying by what death he would glorify God. And when He had spoken this, He said to him, "Follow Me." (John 21:15–19)

In these words spoken by Jesus after His resurrection, Peter seems to finally have discovered who he was and where he was to stand to represent his King. He would never again deny his Lord, not when he was jailed and threatened and probably beaten, not even when standing before the very leaders who had condemned Jesus to death. As he told them to their faces, "Whether it is right in the sight of God to listen to you more than to God, you judge. For we cannot but speak the things which we have seen and heard" (Acts 4:19–20).

When people come to terms with their identity, they know why they've been put on the earth and what they were put here to do. Identity is a revelation of why we were created and what we were created for. It is the place of peace and rest we are told of throughout the New Testament in passages like this:

> Be anxious for nothing, but in everything by prayer and supplication, with thanksgiving, let your requests be made known to God; and the peace of God, which surpasses all understanding, will guard your hearts and minds through Christ Jesus.
>
> Finally, brethren, whatever things are true, whatever things are noble, whatever things are just, whatever things are pure, whatever things are lovely, whatever things are of good report, if there is any virtue and if there is anything praiseworthy—meditate on these things. The things which you learned and received and heard and saw in me, these do, and the God of peace will be with you. (Philippians 4:6–9)

Those who are anxious and restless are only so because they do not yet know who they are. Those who understand and accept their true identity have the key to peace.

The ancient Greek mathematician Archimedes famously said, "Give me a place to stand, and I shall move the earth." Paul said something similar in Ephesians 6:13–14: "Having done all . . . stand." That place to stand is our identity in Christ, which is our heritage. It is the place where we cannot be moved, where we fear nothing but God, and it is the place from which we do not fall back. When we know who we are and have the lever of purpose, we can indeed move the world.

But none of us start out knowing that place.

For my part, I was born at 10:55 in the morning on May 11, 1955, in a Catholic hospital in Los Angeles, California. (Notice all the fives? Five is the number of grace—and I would need a lot of it in the years to come.) I was a colicky baby, probably because I'm allergic to milk, and I cried and screamed constantly.

Not sure what to do with me, the nuns put me in a room reserved for the "bad babies." I lived in that room for the first six months of my life, until Raymond and Rita Landry came to the hospital looking to adopt. Ray had been raised Catholic and Rita was Jewish.

In the process of looking around the nursery, Ray and Rita walked past the room I was in. "What about those babies in there?" Rita asked.

The nun escorting them around said, "Oh, those are the bad babies. You don't want any of them."

Rita was a strong, independent Jewish mother who was not easily intimidated by others, even the nuns. She was tough and open for any challenge. "No, I want to go in there," she told the nun. And before the sister could say anything further, Rita marched into the room.

They later told me that when my mother picked me up, I stopped crying. The nun was amazed. "That's the first time this baby has stopped crying in six months," she told them.

It seemed meant to be. My new parents left with me that day.

They never hid the fact that I was adopted, and I never felt they treated me differently from my natural-born older sister. When they introduced me to people—"This is our son. He's adopted"— the adoption part was never a negative. They always treated it like a special thing. They had *chosen* me, after all. This sense of being special was a big part of my early identity. It was also a reason I didn't really wonder much about my biological parents as I grew up. I was always very happy and loved being a Landry.

My adoptive father, Ray, grew up in Rhode Island. His parents were both alcoholics, and he remembered being left out in the car alone, even in the middle of winter, while they would go into bars and drink. When he was eighteen, he joined the marines to fight in World War II. He did some boxing during his time in the marines, and he must have had leadership potential, because they promoted him to master sergeant and sent his platoon to land on the beach at Guadalcanal. Their mission was to take the Japanese airbase there. During that struggle a Japanese bomb landed so close to his platoon that the explosion blew them out of their foxholes and killed everyone but him. He got malaria, survived that as well, then was reassigned to another group and sent back to Guadalcanal. This time the fighting got so heavy that the navy had to abandon them on the island and they were left to survive on their own. He would never tell us any more than that.

The mix of being in the military and having had a rough childhood made Ray a disciplined father, though. He had promised himself things would be different for his kids. He was going to be the opposite of his parents. He was a blue-collar guy, but he was home every afternoon at five to spend time with us. He never let anything get in the way of that, and I think he even turned down a promotion or two to keep that promise. We always ate dinner together as a family. I can never remember a time when he told us we were going to do something that he didn't follow through on his word. His wife and children were everything to him.

My adoptive mother, Rita, also grew up with alcoholic parents, and her father was abusive. After her parents divorced, she was raised by her aunt, who was blind. My great aunt was a very devout religious person and very protective of my mother. She was always afraid something would happen to her. My mother was very athletic and a lightning-fast swimmer. She trained to be in the Olympics when she was seventeen and was going to swim the English Channel as part of the training, but that plan was shelved when World War II started and my great aunt refused to sign the release for her to go. This totally discouraged my mother. When she grew up, she reacted to her upbringing in the same way my father did. Things were going to be different for her kids, and as a result we were always participating in some kind of athletics or outdoor activities.

The neighborhood where I grew up was made up mostly of Catholic and Jewish families, so our family fit right in. We lived in southern Los Angeles in an area known as Westchester, right on the edge of Inglewood. We were inner-city people, so we grew up with a lot of cultural diversity around us. My father wouldn't tolerate any kind of racism or racial slurs, even though there was a lot of prejudice in some of the homes around us. When kids came to our house—which they did a lot because we had one of the only pools in the neighborhood—they learned to be careful about what they said. Most of the neighborhood learned to swim in our pool, taught by my mom.

It was a magical time to grow up in Los Angeles in the 1960s. It was a time when you ate dinner wherever you happened to be at dinnertime, whether you were at home or at a friend's. It was still safe enough that we could ride our bikes between friends' houses and hitchhike to the beach, which was only five miles away. We went there every day during summer vacation. My mom didn't work outside the home, so we'd put on our suits, she'd load up the station wagon, and off we'd go. Then in the afternoon we'd come home. She'd use the garden hose to spray off all the sand, and then we'd swim in the pool until dusk. That was every day. It was fabulous.

Another thing we did every summer was go on a two-week vacation. Again, we'd load up the station wagon, pile in, and drive somewhere far away. My dad's parents had cleaned up their lives by this time and quit drinking, so they'd often join us. Landry, as you might know, is a French name; my great-grandparents had French Canadian backgrounds, so we called them Mémé and Pépé in the French tradition.

We went as far as New York City in 1964, when the World's Fair was held there. Two years before that, we drove to Seattle for the World's Fair there. We drove all over the country. By the time I was

twelve, we had crisscrossed the United States five or six times. We
visited the Grand Canyon, Florida, and Washington, DC. And all
that travel really helped with my education.

My siblings and I attended St. Jerome's parochial school. It was
a highly respected institution in the city and was considered to be
one of the better schools in the 90045 zip code, so it pulled kids
from all over the city and from all kinds of backgrounds. Built in
the Spanish style, it looked like a classic California mission, with
a red tile roof complete with a steeple. Like all Catholic schools at
the time, it was run mostly by nuns dressed in habits who ruled
like emperors. It was always Reverend Sister so-and-so, Monsignor
such-and-such, and Father so-and-so. We grew up with a strong
sense of history and skirted the rules at our own peril. The teachers
did not hesitate to use the paddle or a ruler across your knuckles.

That was also a time when labeling children by their abilities
was big in schools. It was sort of an educational triage: you had the
smart kids who could figure out most of the stuff on their own,
the middle group who could do well with a little help, and the
remedial kids, who needed a great deal of help but weren't considered worth wasting class time on. If they wanted to do better, it
was up to them to seek out help from their parents or make some
kind of after-hours arrangement with individual teachers. It's not
hard to see how getting one of these labels could create a cycle
that either helped or hurt.

When I was in the first grade, unbeknownst to my parents,
teachers, or myself, I badly needed eyeglasses—in fact, my eye-
sight was so poor that my very first prescription was for bifocal
lenses. St. Jerome's almost always sat us alphabetically, which put
me in the back of the room that year. Each classroom was outfit-
ted with a large green chalkboard in the front, with the alphabet
on display across the wall above it. From my back-row seat, I could
not see the alphabet, so I had difficulty reproducing the letters

and pronouncing their sounds correctly as they were pointed to. Because of this, I was quickly labeled "remedial."

That label would stick with me until tenth grade—not only in school but in my mind. It affected how I carried myself and shaped everyone's expectations for me. Being remedial in school meant the most I could hope for was a remedial job and a remedial future. I assumed I was destined to be below average. And I acted accordingly—goofing off, never trying too hard. After all, if I got my hopes up too high, I might end up disappointed.

One of the ways I dealt with the personal pain of not feeling smart enough was to funnel my energy into being funny. I embraced the identity of the class clown—and I was good at it. The ability to make people laugh made me popular at school, even though the humor covered my own personal shame of not being considered smart.

But one day all that changed. In tenth grade I was over at a girlfriend's house, and her mother, Delores, challenged me. She balked when I told her I was remedial. Delores was a progressive, outspoken Jewish woman who wrote for *Redbook* magazine and whose husband was a dentist. They were people with money who knew how to be successful. So as you can imagine, what she thought made an impression on me.

Delores told me I really was smart but had been misunderstood, and she challenged me to apply myself. "Look," she said, "just give it one semester. Don't skip classes. Listen to what your teachers are saying. Apply yourself to all your assignments. You can be anything you want if you just try. You owe it to yourself to see what is possible if you stop wasting your time."

Thank the Lord I heeded her words. During the next semester all my grades improved tremendously, as did my self-esteem. For the first time in my life, I began to see my potential. A label applied and a label removed changed my perception of who I was and who I could become.

To this day I am grateful for Delores's words of wisdom. She challenged the false identity I had accepted without question. I was not stupid. I was not remedial. I simply needed glasses, and I needed to apply myself.

I didn't give up being the class clown, though, since that was still how I got a lot of attention. That ability to make people laugh was still a pleasant part of my identity and would serve me well in years to come. Where others saw high pressure and big stakes, I could usually find a way to make jokes and ease the tension.

All these things helped form my identity as a young adult—my natural identity anyway: growing up in Southern California in the 1950s and '60s, getting into rock and roll and then folk music as a teen, pitching in Little League, rooting for the Dodgers (and especially for my hero Sandy Koufax), riding motocross, and being raised in a secular household that had muffled Catholic and Jewish influence; my mom putting on a catcher's gear and catching for me as I stood on the mound and threw the ball over the plate that my dad had set up in the backyard; and coming to understand that I had more say in determining my destiny than others had originally allowed. All these things still influence me today, though it's been decades since I've lived in Southern California.

The same is true for all of us. The neighborhood we grew up in, where we went to school, what sports we played or clubs we joined, who our friends were, where we attended (or didn't attend) church or synagogue, the nationalities of our parents and grandparents, and so many other influences together create a heritage that influences who we one day become. For the most part, none of these things are good or bad, they just are. Part of us will always reflect the culture that surrounded us when we were young.

Other important influences are more intentional, based on the decisions and commitments of people who raised us. What our parents allowed us to talk about around the dinner table, what friends we were allowed to have, how (and whether) we spent time as a family, how we were disciplined, what we were allowed to say about others, how birthdays and other holidays were celebrated, what stories were told at family gatherings, how connected we were to our extended family—such experiences, based on decisions made by the adults in our lives, feed the formation of our natural identities. Good parents make conscious decisions rather than just leaving the formation of their children's identities to chance.

I'm so glad Ray Landry made the choice to be a family man and put us first, before work or anything else. That commitment is an important part of my natural heritage, a great foundational influence in my life. So was his work ethic, his intolerance of racism, and his insistence on respect for my mother. There were other influences from Ray, such as his blue-collar perspective and how he felt about wealthy people, which I later had to overcome to be successful in business. But overall I'm extremely grateful for what was provided for me as a child and for the way I was raised. There was so much more good than bad, and what my adoptive parents have given me was so different from what I would have experienced had I grown up in an orphanage. Even if I was given a chance to go back in a time machine and "fix" any of it, there isn't much I would change.

One of the difficulties of identity, however, is that so much of what shapes us is beyond anyone's conscious control. In many ways, in fact, a child's formation through childhood is an almost completely unconscious process. And considering the kinds of trauma many children experience—poverty, abuse, bullying and belittling, abandonment, parental divorce or addiction—it's amazing that any of us turn out well at all. But there's no question that these experiences, too, shape our identities.

Some aspects of our identities seem to be sown into the very fabric of our DNA. We inherit them from our families, just as we inherit our eye color or body type. As an adoptee, I'm acutely aware of this reality. I wish I had a nickel for every time my adoptive father said, "I just don't know where Curtis gets this"—speaking of some trait, some food preference, or some hobby that called to me but didn't interest him in the slightest. Decades later, when I met my biological father, I would learn that I shared many of those traits or preferences or interests with him or with someone else in my biological family tree.

All these factors—what we inherit from our birth parents, what we are taught at home, what we pick up from our environment, what happens to us, and what we choose for ourselves—combine to shape our natural identities. Yet, at the same time, every one of us also has a spiritual identity. This is the purpose God created us for, the person God created us to become. This is our true identity—a gift God had in mind for each of us long before we were born. As He told Jeremiah:

> Before I formed you in the womb I knew you;
> Before you were born I sanctified you.
>
> (JEREMIAH 1:5)

Our spiritual identity is placed deep within us, and it doesn't come out by accident. It's something we have to discover, step into, and manifest. It demands choosing to see ourselves from the perspective of heaven and overcoming the influences of the world around us.

This, of course, is our deepest and most authentic identity. It is the key to living out our true selves. Unfortunately, it can easily be confused or counterfeited when our priorities get out of order.

I struggled with this throughout my life, but at a much greater degree when I left my parents' house and wandered out into the world to make my own way.

three

THE COUNTERFEIT SELF

> But you have not so learned Christ, if indeed you
> have heard Him and have been taught by Him, as the
> truth is in Jesus: that you put off, concerning your
> former conduct, the old man which grows corrupt
> according to the deceitful lusts, and be renewed in
> the spirit of your mind, and that you put on the new
> man which was created according to God, in true
> righteousness and holiness.
>
> —EPHESIANS 4:20–24

AFTER I GRADUATED FROM HIGH SCHOOL, I moved
to Lake Tahoe because I wanted to learn how to snow ski. I got
a job at one of the casinos there, and through some dumb luck

and because I was a hard worker I ended up working on the nine-teenth floor, which was where the entertainers and high rollers stayed. My time there proved to be quite an experience. It made me comfortable hanging around with famous and wealthy people and taught me a lot of things that would shape my life for years to follow. I think many of the traits that later helped me to become a top salesman were acquired there. But so were others, like a false sense of what success looked like and what it meant to be happy, as well as a few habits that almost got me killed.

It wasn't long before I was making twice as much as my dad had ever made, and I thought I had arrived. I was chauffeuring VIPs around, attending swanky parties, and had access to areas most of the other twenty-three hundred employees didn't. I thought I was living the high life, and I was only nineteen.

Then one day I was parked by the front door waiting for some-one, and I saw this girl walking toward the building that housed Human Resources. She had strawberry-blond hair that hung all the way down her back and a pair of those short shorts that were so popular in the 1970s. She was beautiful. I was pretty sure she was going in to apply for a job, and I wanted to get a chance to talk to her before anyone else.

I started the van, pulled over to where she was, and asked if she needed any help. She was fine, she told me, then spun on her heels and walked into the building.

Strike one.

Of course, they hired her, and I found out a little more about her during the next few weeks. Her name was Christie, and she was from Oklahoma. At that time the casino had a prefer-ence for wholesome girls from the Midwest and the South. They were pretty, naturally polite, and knew how to carry themselves around ornery men.

That fit Christie perfectly. She'd come to Tahoe to get over a guy she'd broken up with back home, which was probably why she said no each of the next fifteen times I asked her out.

Strike two.

Then one night I was working the graveyard shift. It was about three in the morning and I was on call, hanging out with the headliner—who happened to be B.B. King that night—between shows. (Casinos never sleep, after all.) B.B. had one more show to do, then I was done for the night. So I called Christie. She worked days but surprisingly she was still awake. "Listen," I pleaded, "I really need to meet you. I think if we just go out one time—," I caught my breath. "Listen, there's one more show tonight. I need to sit through it and get the headliner back up to his room, then be sure he goes to bed. Come sit with me during the show and we can talk. I'll be down front."

Surprisingly, she agreed.

It turned out she was the easiest person in the world to talk to, and we poured out our hearts to each other during that show. Christie became my wife, and we've been together ever since.

No strike three.

A casino is no place to keep a steady relationship though. With twenty-three hundred employees, half of them women and all of them beautiful, and a constant party atmosphere, being in a faithful, long-term relationship was not on the menu. Christie and I knew that. We were in love and wanted to build a life together, but our chances of doing that while working at the Tahoe casino were pretty slim. So Christie decided to take me home to meet her family.

You can imagine the reception we got—bringing a Southern California guy to the Sooner State. A guy from the land of surfing, movie stars, and orchards to the backbone of the nation, the state of wheat, corn, and oil drilling. It was the difference between a sunburned face from being at the beach all day and a sunburned back of the neck from working in the fields from sunup to sundown.

Then add in the fact that Christie's dad was a bail bondsman, worked with the police every day, and had a reputation in the community as a straight shooter. He was politically connected, had a flattop haircut, wore pointy-toed cowboy boots, smoked a cigar he chewed hard on, and looked down at everyone over the top of his reading glasses. The first time I met him, I wasn't sure I was going to survive.

I think, instead, he decided to let someone else finish me off. "As a favor," he put in a word with a friend and helped me get a job—the hardest job he could find in five states. The company built storm shelters and needed a welder. Nothing like running a welding torch and moving huge pieces of metal plating around in one-hundred-degree heat and 80 percent humidity. I'm pretty sure he didn't think I'd last long. The man who owned the company also had a reputation for working his guys to death, and most of them, to put it mildly, had no great love for hippies from Southern Cal. I was lucky on several occasions not to have ended up in a fistfight.

But I worked hard at that job and refused to quit. I'd show up at Christie's granny's house at six in the morning for breakfast, where they'd do things like kill a rabbit for breakfast and fry it up in bacon grease with eggs. Can you imagine what that was like for a kid who'd grown up in a place that was like Disneyland? Let alone being the kefir-drinking health foodie my ex-girlfriend's mother, Dolores, had influenced me to be? It was certainly a different world.

Of course, Christie also met my parents. I was nervous because my mother had never liked any of the girls I dated growing up. When she met Christie, though, she had only one thing to say, and she said it right in front of Christie. She told me, "She's too good for you." There was no higher praise from my mom. I knew I had to make this work.

So eventually, back in Oklahoma, I did. One day my boss called Christie's dad and told him, "Doc, listen. I'm doing everything I can, but the kid just keeps working. I can't give him anything harder to do. He just won't quit!"

I'd passed the test.

Not too long after that, Christie and I got married and eventually settled down in her hometown. Since it was evident by now that I wasn't going anywhere, her father connected me with a life and health insurance salesman in the area in the hope that he'd teach me about the business.

During the next seven years I became the number-one salesperson in Oklahoma for three different insurance companies. I worked hard, learned the craft of insurance sales by studying every night at home, and specialized in selling to hospitals, doctors, and municipalities. I closed so many deals on the golf course that within three years we bought a house on the course and became regular members of the country club. I'd been told I would never be able to prosper in that town if I didn't join the First Baptist Church. I considered it, but I had seen how many of the churchgoers behaved behind closed doors at the country club and figured I could do without the hypocrisy. So I declined to become a Baptist—and succeeded in my business anyway.

Because of my success and Christie's dad's connections, some people in town started priming me for politics. Every time there was a big event in town, I was supposed to be out schmoozing with the movers and shakers. I was making a name for myself. We were out at the country club almost every Friday night. I thought I was climbing the ladder of success.

God had other plans though.

One night, out of nowhere, Christie decided she wanted to

go to church. This was shortly after our daughter, Megann, was born. Christie came into the living room and asked me if she could go to church.

"Sure, I don't care," I told her. "It's fine with me." It seemed a little weird, but if she wanted to go, I didn't see anything wrong with it.

It was a weeknight service, so Christie left Megann with me and went to church. That night Christie got radically saved. And it didn't happen at the Baptist church that would have gotten me some credit in the community. She got saved at a Pentecostal church that most of the people I knew dismissed as "holy rollers."

Suddenly Christie didn't want to hang out at the country club anymore. So I went alone, and in a small town it doesn't take long for people to figure out why I was on my own. "Where's Christie?" they'd ask. And then, "Oh, that's right. She doesn't like to be around drinking. She's probably at church rolling on the floor with the Holy Ghost."

I felt like Jesus had stolen my wife.

But the tough thing was, I couldn't get mad at Christie for any of this, because she'd suddenly become an even better wife. She was calmer and more peaceful. She didn't preach at me or try to coerce me into going to church with her. She just loved me, took great care of Megann, and kept everything running smoothly in our home. Sometimes she'd mention offhand that she was praying for me, but that was it. It was hard to complain about.

Then the man who had hired me at the insurance company died of leukemia. Two years earlier he'd remarried, and after his death we learned that he'd put everything in his new wife's name. The company structure changed so drastically as a result that it no longer worked for me. I knew I could fight for what had been promised to me, but that would mean a lot of legal expenses, which seemed crazy at the time. I also could have started my own office with the clients I had, but that would have created too much political fallout, and that didn't feel right either.

I was conflicted. If I stayed, whatever I did would make a big stink in the community and ultimately reflect back on Christie's family. We decided it was time to move on.

I learned that a large and established stock brokerage firm wanted to expand their business into the life insurance sector. I contacted them, and the general manager hired me to introduce the value of life insurance into wealthy clients' financial portfolios. Christie and I were extremely excited about this opportunity. We sold our house in Oklahoma and moved to the Seattle area. But when I arrived at the office for my new job, I discovered that the general manager who had hired me had been transferred to New York. The new GM wanted nothing to do with life insurance or with any new venture; in fact, he was determined that my project fail under his watch. And after the funding was pulled, fail it did—big time. In hindsight, I can see this was the beginning of God allowing me to be broken in order to get my attention. I had to learn I could not do everything in my own strength.

After this I was offered a position with a sales training firm, which I enjoyed until the company got into financial trouble, so I had to look elsewhere. I ended up at a job where I did extremely well. I made millions in profit for that company and was financially very well rewarded. I thought I was back on track.

Life at that company reflected stereotypical 1980s excess. For board meetings they would have a five-star restaurant bring in lox and bagels, fresh fruit, and a continental breakfast that would make royalty blush. During the first break in the morning, someone would start laying out lines of cocaine. No one flinched; this was just the way they lived, a privilege of wealth. They were snorting coke, eating gourmet food, making million-dollar deals. They assumed they could do whatever they wanted and no one could call them on it. That was just the world they lived in—and it was my world too.

I had an expense account of $2,500 a month, which I used for taking clients to the nicest restaurants and private clubs in the state and buying tickets for the Sonics, Mariners, and Seahawks. Christie and I owned a house on Green Lake in one of the more desirable neighborhoods in Seattle, and I drove a BMW.

I was living in the fast lane and running with a fast company.

But I still really had no idea who I was.

Like many people in the first half of their lives, I was running hard to define who I was and to make my mark on the world. I was luckier than most because I had a good upbringing and a loving family at home, but I really didn't have anything to live for bigger than myself and my family. From a material success standpoint I was doing well, but my soul was languishing. I was receiving accolades from those around me but had yet to connect with my true purpose, discover my spiritual identity, or plug into my God-given calling.

In fact, rather than doing the hard work of figuring out who I was, I was taking the easy way out—and if I wasn't careful, I was going to die of stress or from drug or alchohol abuse. It's a horrible thing to die before you know who you are and what you're living for.

There's an interesting aspect of identity described in the Hebrew commentaries that I believe is worth exploring here. According to Esther 2:5, "in Shushan the citadel there was a certain Jew whose name was Mordecai the son of Jair, the son of Shimei, the son of Kish, a Benjamite."

This text calls Mordecai "a certain Jew," but it also says his lineage was that of a Benjamite. Though today we tend to confuse being Jewish with being Hebrew, the term *Jew* was originally applied to someone from the tribe of Judah, which was just one of the twelve tribes of Israel, as was the tribe of Benjamin.

So which was it? Was Mordecai a Jew (from the tribe of Judah) or a Benjamite (from the tribe of Benjamin)? If you look at the original language it becomes clear, because the word referring to Mordecai in this passage is *yehudi*. In the Torah, the Jewish term for the first five books of the Bible, it translates as *yudi*. And according to the Mishnah, a Hebrew commentary on the Scriptures, the term didn't only refer to being Judaean but also described anyone who worshipped the one God. By implication, that meant anyone who refused idol worship or, more specifically, anyone who refused to bow down to any god other than the one true God.

In other words, Jews are those who hold to the Shema, a fundamental confession of faith found in Deuteronomy 6:4: "Hear, O Israel: The LORD our God, the LORD is one!"

How is that for an identity woven into the very word that defines one's ethnic heritage? Just as being called an American means standing for individualism and democracy, being a Jew means you're someone who only worships one God, the God of Israel. And to Jewish people who take their heritage seriously, this sense of identity is all-important and often extends in a desire for their children to marry within their culture to preserve the monotheistic covenant for future generations. The covenants their Jewish ancesters made with God are everything to them. Those covenants hold all God's promises for their success and the abundance in their lives. And at the heart of those covenants is that they worship only the one God.

So being called a Jew meant that Mordecai had a reputation for not bowing down to idols. Refusing to worship anything or anyone other than the one God was essential to his identity.

Let me give you another example. Think of the story of Joseph in the Bible. When Joseph was called before Pharaoh to interpret Pharaoh's dream (Genesis 41), he would not bow down before Pharaoh, who had the power of life and death over everyone in the room. Joseph was the only one who wouldn't bend his knee and treat Pharaoh as a god.

Pharaoh must have thought, *Okay, I've heard about you. They told me you don't bow to any god but your own, and I can respect that—if you give me what I want. But you'd better darn well nail this thing because I can't have you coming here in front of my sorcerers and my mystics and my priests, not bowing, not respecting me as a god, and then not having anything better to offer than any of them.*

If Joseph didn't get it right, he was going to die because he wouldn't kneel. But Joseph knew that if he did kneel, there was no way he was going to get it right. He must have thought something along the lines of, *I didn't come this far to give in. My brothers threw me in a pit and wanted to kill me. Potiphar's wife accused me of trying to rape her. I spent thirteen years of my life as a slave and in prison. Now I'm standing here in front of the ruler of all Egypt. God has brought me this far. I'm not going to do anything to compromise putting the one God before anything else.*

That was a big risk. Joseph could have just bowed. Then, if he didn't get the interpretation right, at least he wouldn't be executed. Pharaoh would probably have thrown him back in prison, but at least he'd still be alive.

But of course Joseph didn't bow his knee. And God didn't let him down. God revealed to Joseph what Pharaoh's dreams meant and how the entire Middle East could be saved from the famine the dreams foretold. Joseph became the second-most-powerful person in the land of Egypt because he refused to take the easy way out of idolatry and break the covenant his ancestors had made.

Stories like that permeate the Jewish heritage. Through the centuries, they have defined the Jewish identity. And that's why, in the midst of the Holocaust, Jews in concentration camps risked their lives to get a candle and to light it for the Sabbath. That's why they observed the Jewish holy days in the camps. They couldn't forget who they were, and they refused to let their oppressors control the annual rhythm of their heritage and devotion. After all, without those observances, what would they be? How else would God know they were honoring Him above all else—even above life itself? How could God rescue them if they didn't honor His covenants with them?

But none of that was part of how I grew up. Even though my adoptive father was Catholic and my adoptive mother was Jewish, they didn't share those aspects of my heritage with me. Culturally speaking, I was raised a Gentile and didn't know not to put anything else before God in defining who I was or who I was becoming. So I grew up to worship at the altar of success, finding my identity in the amount of money in my bank account, the size of my home, and the kind of car I drove, and accepting that happiness and "really living" consisted of all the excesses that went with those things.

Now, I didn't literally bow down before those tokens of success. Americans today don't usually do that kind of thing. But I did give them my all. I was so dedicated to having them that I would do anything to keep from being separated from them. If that's not a description of worship, I don't know what is.

Do you see the connection here between worship and identity? Who we are is defined by who or what we worship—who or what we put first in our lives and invest our lives in.

In our time on the earth, we human beings only have three things we can give or invest: our time, our talents, and our treasures. For me back then, all three of those were invested in my career and in trying to keep up with the people I worked with. I was constructing my identity according to the false god of success, what I owned, and the experiences I could afford that most others couldn't.

Jewish heritage tells us that nothing in life is worth that. There is only one God, and He is not money or fame or influence or travel or hobbies or sports or anything else. Those things can be used and enjoyed, but our time, talents, and treasure are to be dedicated to something more valuable. If we don't do that, we are worshipping idols.

Idolatry is when we worship anything that we can make or have made with our own hands, as Romans 1:22–23 describes vividly: "Professing to be wise, [the ungodly] became fools, and changed the glory of the incorruptible God into an image made like corruptible man—and birds and four-footed animals and creeping things."

An idol can indeed be something as tangible as a statue, as was common in Bible times. But it can also be something as intangible as a career or hobby, especially today. It is really anything we use to define ourselves above our relationship with God.

The journey of chasing a counterfeit identity can be painful and expensive—not only financially but primarily in relationships and destiny. If we don't know who we really are, it's hard to sincerely connect with others. We end up hanging around with those who are as lost as we are, and rejection can feel like a way of life. We sense something is missing in each other and find it difficult to trust, and then not having anyone to trust only leads to more brokenness. How can we know how to relate to others when we don't even know how to relate to ourselves? And how can we know who we were meant to be until we connect with the God who made us? That's the only way to find fulfillment, satisfaction, peace, and purpose in our lives.

Idolatry is a spirit that is never satisfied. It requires more and more until it sucks every last drop out of its victim. It consumes all our time and attention until we find ourselves wondering: *What am I doing? How did I get here? Is this really who I am?*

For me, those questions came one night when God caught up with me at 120 miles an hour.

four

AMBUSHED BY
THE TRUTH

*You shall know the truth, and the truth shall make
you free.*

—John 8:32

I WAS DRIVING HOME from a business meeting in Tacoma,
Washington, to our home in Issaquah, which is about forty miles
across Lake Washington from Seattle. I was drunk, high on
cocaine, and had no idea how fast I was going. When I saw the
police lights flashing behind me—red and blue spinning in my
rearview mirror—I panicked. I knew if I got pulled over, a DUI
would be the least of my worries. In complete and utter foolish-
ness, I decided to outrun the officer. I was driving a 5 Series BMW.
How would he ever catch me?

You don't think that way when you are sober, of course. But I was nothing close to sober.

It was true there was no way the policeman could catch me if I didn't slow down. But he had a radio, and his wasn't the only police car in the state of Washington. When I got closer to home, I was sure I had evaded him. I slowed down. Then, as I approached the entryway to our subdivision, an officer appeared out of (seemingly) nowhere and motioned me to the side of the road.

There was no escape now. I had nowhere else to go. I pulled over, opened my car door, and extended both of my arms so the officer could cuff me. Looking at me, he asked me something I'll never forget.

"What are you doing?"

I responded with deep truth and a confession: "I don't know what I'm doing."

He just looked at me. "Do you live in this neighborhood?"

"Yes, sir. I do."

He looked around at the houses near the entryway, then back at me. "I am going to follow you to your home," he said, "and I sure hope you do actually live here." Then he walked back to his car, which I saw for the first time in the shadows.

I was shocked. I put my arms down, climbed back into my car, closed the door, and started to drive—slowly and carefully. I almost jumped out of my skin when the officer flicked on his lights before following. By then it must have been early in the morning. It was surreal seeing the quiet streets and my neighbors' windows flashing blue and red.

I found myself desperately praying under my breath that my garage-door opener would work. Thankfully it did, and I parked my car as the officer waited.

Still unsure what was happening, I walked out of the garage to talk to the officer.

"Young man," he told me, "I don't know why I am doing this, but I am going to let you go. I would encourage you to do some deep thinking about the direction your life is going."

I can only imagine what the expression on my face must have been. "Yes, sir," I said as respectfully as I could—suddenly glad for the manners and respect for authority I'd learned in Oklahoma. "Thank you, sir."

I turned and walked into the house. As I reached to close the garage door, my hand was shaking. Then I felt my entire body tremble from head to heels. In that instant, I was completely sober.

All the lights were off in the house. Thankfully both Christie and Megann were sound asleep. I was grateful neither had woken. I took off my shoes, made my way quietly down the hall, and then eased down on the edge of the bed. The red and blue flashing lights were gone, and I was sure the officer had pulled away, but his words were still with me, *Young man, I would encourage you to do some deep thinking about the direction your life is going.*

I tried to make sense of all that had just transpired and the grace that had been extended to me. What was I doing? Where had my success taken me? I suddenly felt very lucky to still be alive.

Christie stirred behind me. "Oh, you're home," she said. Then, suddenly confused by why I was sitting there in the dark, she reached over toward me. "Are you okay?"

"I think God just saved me from ruining my life," I told her.

As I look back now, roughly thirty years later, I realize that a lot of my outlandish behavior—which could be a book of its own—had been my misguided way of searching for purpose and identity. I'd been trying to accomplish something I thought could be calculated in dollar signs and experiences available only to the wealthiest and most elite. I'd been going 120 miles an hour, thinking only about how much fun I was having and how important I was. But suddenly, in a flash of red and blue lights, the shallowness and meaninglessness of everything I had been chasing had been exposed.

That night a part of me died to my false identity, goals, and aspirations. I don't know how else to say it, but the mistress of power and achievement had failed me. That night I knew I needed to end our affair. I just wasn't sure how to do it yet—because who would I be then?

Over the years I had searched for personal identity through music, motocross, rubbing elbows with the rich and famous, earning big paychecks, impressing people, and consuming drugs and alcohol—but I hadn't fully understood what I was doing. I realized that after all that time, I didn't know anything. I didn't know God, I didn't know me, and I had no idea why I'd been put on the earth.

Up to that point, I had been subconsciously trying to cover the pain of not knowing my true identity. My mischievous behavior in high school had been a cloak for what was missing on the inside—a sense of who I was and what I was called to be or accomplish. Moving away from my family to Lake Tahoe had been an attempt to make my own mark on the world and run away from my lack of identity in Los Angeles. Then getting into sales and finding a way to make the big bucks had been yet another attempt to fill the void inside me with something external, as if things could fill up the hole in my soul. Still shaking, sitting on the edge of my bed, I got my first glimpse of that truth.

True identity is the taproot of every soul. If we have a healthy connection with that root and know our true identity, our lives will bear fruit in line with our calling and purpose. But detachment from our identity taproot will yield stunted fruit or even turn our souls into dried-out firewood.

That night it seemed clear to me that all the fruit I had borne thus far in my life was bitter and devoid of any lasting value. Something drastically needed to change, but at that point, I wasn't quite sure what. I just knew there was something more.

When I woke up the next morning, I was still trembling from my encounter with the officer and the truth about myself the encounter had revealed. (Looking back, the only thing that makes sense to me is that the officer was not a man, but an angel sent by God to rescue me from my own self-destruction.) I still wasn't that clear about what had happened or what I needed to do next. I just knew I had been given fair warning.

I went back to work that day rattled but still a mostly unchanged man. The drugs and alcohol had lost some of their appeal, and I decided I needed to be more careful with them for a bit. Otherwise I continued my high-octane lifestyle. But I also had a deep sense there was something more out there than this race to collect all the toys you can before you die. My encounter with the officer had created a hunger for truth that would not let me go.

God built that longing and love for truth into human nature. It's one of our foundational drives, and there is an innate desire in every soul to search it out, especially when we've gotten off course and caught up in false identities. We may not know exactly what we're looking for, but we're pretty sure that what we have now isn't it.

When we finally do find the truth, it breaks through confusion and not only sets us free but also strengthens our character and our resolve. But before then, when we are insecure or unsure whether something is the full truth, we tend to fight everything and anyone. So often we argue with others, but we are ultimately arguing with ourselves. The disagreement becomes a debate as our soul tries to decipher what we truly believe. And meanwhile our souls languish in unrest, trying to do what they do best—finding comfort in a safe harbor, a place of rest, a place of truth:

> Truly my soul silently waits for God;
> From Him comes my salvation.
> He only is my rock and my salvation;
> He is my defense;
> I shall not be greatly moved.
>
> (PSALM 62:1–2)

I didn't know it at the time, but that's exactly what my soul was seeking that night the officer stopped me and then let me go. But it would take another year for me to find it.

I was home alone after closing a big deal at work. Christie and Megann were visiting family in Oklahoma. One of the promises I had made to her parents was that if we moved to Washington, at least the two of them would come back to visit every year. So the girls often left Washington in the late summer to spend a few weeks at Christie's parents' lake house.

Business was at an all-time high. We'd just bought another new home with room for our two BMWs in the garage. I had exceeded the goals I'd set for myself and had just been told that my department had made a record number of sales for the year. I was up for a huge bonus and was going to be employee of the year. We had season tickets on the fifty-yard line in the Kingdome, premier seating at the Super Sonic games, and I was on a first name basis with the maître d' at many of the finest restaurants in Seattle. Businesswise, everything was going my way.

It was a Friday, and I had dropped Christie and Megann off at SeaTac International Airport that morning. On the way home, I stopped at my favorite wine shop to treat myself to a bottle of

Cristal champagne. My plan was to put on my favorite jazz music and relax in the Jacuzzi of our master suite to celebrate me and my so-called success.

When I got home, I turned on the jazz, filled the tub with hot water, and with a sense of deserving a little extra pampering, added some of Christie's bath oil. I climbed in and poured some of the champagne into a crystal flute. I set the glass on the ledge next to the tub, the bottle into a bucket of ice, sank into the water, and closed my eyes.

That was when I felt it—the foreboding sense that someone had come up behind me in the room. For some reason I couldn't turn my head around to look, but anxiety began to grip every muscle of my body. The water was hot and soothing, the music was soft, the bubbles were tiny perfection—and still I felt myself slipping into a panic.

I remember putting my hands on my face, trying to get hold of myself. What was wrong with me? I hadn't even had a drink of the Cristal yet. There was a knob for the music on the wall by the tub, so I turned it off, hoping silence would help. It didn't. I put my hands to my face again, and when I took them away it was like there was a tiny movie screen in front of me at about faucet level. It began showing flashes of my past—flashes of things I had done that I was anything but proud of, things I hoped no one would ever find out about.

I still didn't know who the figure behind me was, but as I watched each event, I felt how deeply they had hurt Him.

My mouth formed the words "I didn't mean to hurt you" over and over again at each image on the screen. And they weren't just words. I truly felt His pain and disappointment, and I was truly sorry. The more I repented, the more I feared looking back over my shoulder at the figure.

I now know, of course, that a visitation of the Lord was

standing beside me in my brokenness. To this day, I don't know how long events ran over that screen, but I do know that when I entered the tub, the water was as hot as I could stand it, and when I got out, the water was cold. My feet and my hands were wrinkled like raisins.

I didn't just weep or cry in that tub. I travailed. The only other time I have cried in such a way was when my mother, Rita, died. The emotional pain I experienced while watching that screen was not pain or guilt or anxiety over being caught. It came from feeling what Jesus had experienced as a result of my every selfish action and cruel choice. I realized that He had always been there, He'd never left me a moment in my life, and so I had dragged Him through every one of my darkest moments.

The remorse and heaviness I was experiencing was not condemnation; it was conviction for hurting the heart of Jesus. It is very difficult for me to put this into words, but as I look back so many years later, I think it was a spiritual experience of intercession for my own life. I was sharing in the sufferings of the Messiah for the unsaved me—from the time I was very small up until that very moment. And at the same time, I had an incredible sense of the Father's love and of the love of Jesus in the midst of my poor choices. Even though I had done all these horrible things, He had loved me and never rejected me. I personally experienced the unconditional love of God, and I would never be the same again.

When I got out of the Jacuzzi, my voice was hoarse and raspy, and I felt emotionally and physically exhausted. Yet somehow, on the inside, I felt completely refreshed. I was weak, but I felt an inner strength as I was cleansed and forgiven by God. I never did work up the courage to look over my left shoulder, but I know it was Jesus standing there—once again never leaving me.

The cold bathwater had chilled me so much that I had to take a hot shower to warm up. I didn't know what to do next, so I called Christie in Oklahoma. After briefly sharing with her about what happened, I said, "I think I just had a nervous breakdown."

I heard her crying on the other end of the line, then her tears gave way to laughter. "You didn't have a breakdown," she said, hardly able to get the words out through joyful giggles. "You just got *saved!*"

I was perplexed. "Saved from what?" I asked. She just giggled some more.

Though I wouldn't find out until after she got home, Christie had been praying steadily for me for years without saying a word. She'd never nagged me to go to church with her and Megann. She'd never poked at me about my drinking or drug abuse. Instead, in obedience to the Lord's instruction, Christie had felt led to love me toward the kingdom. When she got home and knew I was finally receptive, she felt released to share the full message of salvation.

As she did, I finished what was started in the tub. I gave my life to Christ. Doing so filled my heart with a sense of purpose and a new sense of who I was. My identity had been transformed in a miraculous way and to an extent I would only discover in the days to come.

five

A NEW CREATION

> *Therefore, if anyone is in Christ, he is a new
> creation; old things have passed away; behold, all
> things have become new.*
>
> —2 CORINTHIANS 5:17

IN THE DAYS FOLLOWING my tub experience, I spent a
great amount of time in deep introspection, trying to figure
out what had just happened to me and what this transformation
meant going forward. All I knew for sure was that something had
changed—everything had changed, in fact. I had this irrepress-
ible joy. I had a sense that something was on the horizon, but I
couldn't yet make it out.

When I went to work on Monday, coworkers kept looking at
me strangely. "You look different. What happened to you?" they
asked. As I tried to share what had happened, they got extremely
uncomfortable. It's kind of funny in hindsight. I was really flipping

them out. But I couldn't help myself. After I had told a couple of people, I couldn't wait to share it with everyone in the office.

Everyone should have this! I thought.

But none of them were ready for it.

At the end of the following week, the company president called me into his office. He sat at his desk, and I stood in front of him. He never offered me the chance to sit down.

"Look," he said, "I hired you to increase sales for our company, and you have, for which I am grateful. But I didn't hire you to be some kind of Jesus freak. I hired you to be a sales manager—period."

He squirmed in his chair a little, and his eyes dropped to his desk. "I'm terminating your employment contract, effective immediately. You'll get severance, but not your bonus. I'm sorry, but that's the board's decision. There's nothing I can do about it."

Finally looking up again, he said, "That's all. Clean out your desk and be out of the office before noon."

And that was it. The month I was up to be employee of the year was the month I was fired.

I was stunned, to say the least. I had just been introduced to my new identity in Christ, and almost immediately everything that had made me me was gone. I'd worked since I was eleven years old, and being successful was part of who I was. Now I had no job. No income. No bonus.

God wasn't exactly easing me into my new life. In a matter of weeks it was out of the old and into the new. I was either going to stand with Him or fall flat on my face.

I left the office shaken and unsure of what to do next. I had never been unemployed without another immediate prospect for a job on the horizon. The only thing I could think to do was wait for Christie to pick me up and drive home. (I had to leave the company car behind.)

When I told Christie what had happened, she didn't seem too concerned. "The Lord will provide," she told me. I could not see it or understand it, but she had faith for it. Thank goodness one of us did.

I began actively searching for employment with the firms that had been our competitors, but I had no luck. The company that fired me had spread the word that I was a Jesus freak, and it was tough to even get an interview. It looked like we would indeed have to wait for the Lord to provide.

Looking back on this painful experience, I have concluded that you can't restore personal identity without first dying to the old false identity. Being born again is only a part of that. John 1:12 tells us: "But as many as received Him, to them He gave the right to become children of God, to those who believe in His name."

When you are born again, you embark on a spiritual journey of discovering your purpose and what God created you for. Even though I was thirty-six years old and a mature man when I got saved, I had to start thinking like a child again, because I was suddenly a member of a new family. I didn't know anything about following Jesus or belonging to God. It was like being adopted all over again, but this time as an adult. In order to enjoy this new family of God, I had to learn a new family culture and, more important, understand the wisdom and knowledge of doing things in my new Father's way.

I also had to learn what faith was and how "without faith it is impossible to please Him, for he who comes to God must believe that He is, and that He is a rewarder of those who diligently seek Him" (Hebrews 11:6). When we live for ourselves, we can calculate our risks and choose accordingly, but when we live for God, everything is by faith. This can be very scary for a type-A personality like me, who is used to being self-sufficient, self-providing, and self-protecting. It is hard to let go of the reins of our own lives, but God is a loving God and the Holy Spirit is the Comforter. He will not stretch us further than we can survive in the season we're in, even when it feels like that is exactly what He's doing.

I would learn in time that in His sovereign, creative power, the Lord arranges circumstances that can sometimes appear as troubles or challenges when in fact they are hidden opportunities for us to draw closer to Him. When we overcome battles and trials, the reward is often found in discovering a deeper expression of our place in the family of heaven.

Every call has a beginning, and all our beginnings start with what Paul described in 2 Corinthians 5:17: "If anyone is in Christ, he is a new creation; old things have passed away; behold, all things have become new."

Being born again, in other words, means being baptized into the new and leaving behind the old. For me personally, the experience extended beyond being saved, beyond the fact that my sins were forgiven and I was not going to hell. I immediately had to surrender control over both my life and my livelihood to Jesus as Lord and Savior. I had no choice but to be completely sold out. God had things He wanted me to do, and to accomplish those I needed to spend the remainder of my life living for His purposes. There was no time to waste.

Paul taught the church at Ephesus that God "predestined us to adoption as sons by Jesus Christ to Himself, according to the good pleasure of His will" (Ephesians 1:5). Over the years, I have discovered that the "good pleasure of His will" is usually found in an area that I excel at and is, in fact, part of what He first called me to do. When His pleasure is my pleasure, I experience the enjoyment of being a son and not a slave to being "religiously correct" or obligated.

What I am trying to convey to you is that the dreams and the desires within our hearts, our likes and dislikes and preferences, are all little pieces of a jigsaw puzzle that can help us discover what our true identities look like. But we have to give them to God, and that all begins with the death of the counterfeit.

The assassination of my counterfeit self was exactly what happened that day my boss fired me. God wasn't wasting any more time on the self-important Curt Landry. He had something else for me to do, and that started with me figuring out who the real Provider was in my household. It felt like God had ripped off the bandage and the scab along with it. I felt raw and vulnerable. But I was also very interested in finding out what God had in store for me.

I had never gone to church with Christie and Megann, so when I started showing up for worship every week, people noticed. I knew very little about the Bible and what was in it. My faith was in its infancy. However, the local church women knew Christie as a woman who was on fire for the Lord and full of faith. Sometimes I felt like the prize steer being shown off at the county fair, but the people in that church were very kind and welcoming. We were in the right place for me to grow.

Grace Church in Redmond, on the east side of Lake Washington, was full of young families like ours. Pastor Steve and Julie Gutzler, who are still our friends, were our age and led a church I would refer to as a late 1980s, early 1990s yuppie church. Its membership included Mariner baseball players, business executives, and an abundance of families with young children.

I hadn't attended Grace long before I noticed a young guy named Stan, probably because he drove a brand-new Mercedes Benz sedan. (My adoptive father, Ray, was a car guy, so I always noticed what people drove.) I remember wondering how he'd talked his dad into letting him drive it to church every week. He didn't dress as if he could afford a new car—the guy wore a clip-on tie and tennis shoes to church. The Mercedes didn't seem to fit his quiet, timid demeanor, either. Was he hoping his dad's car would impress someone?

We were at the church just a couple of weeks when Stan walked up to me and asked, "Can you sell apples?"

Oh great, was my first thought, *they must need help with the church bazaar or something.* It wasn't like I was doing anything else though. "Sure," I answered, "I can sell apples. I can sell anything."

I waited for the time and place info on the bazaar, but it never came. Instead, he handed me his card. "Call me and we'll set up a lunch." With that, he turned and walked away.

When we got home from church, I told Christie, "You know that young guy who drives his dad's big Mercedes to church every week? He asked me if I could sell apples for the church bazaar."

Christie nodded, continuing to make lunch. "What did you tell him?"

"I told him, 'Of course I can sell apples!' I was up for employee of the year in sales!"

"That's good," she said, putting toppings on a salad. "And what did he say to that?"

"He handed me his card and said to call him to set up a lunch." I shrugged. "Is that weird or what?"

She shrugged back. "I think you should call him."

So I did. He didn't answer, so I left a message. He left a message in return sometime later. "No. Too busy this week. Call me next week."

I just shook my head.

By the next Sunday nothing had broken on the job front, and I was beginning to feel the weight of the bills piling up. At the end of the service, I saw Stan again. "Don't forget to call me about lunch," he said. He was gone before I could respond. So I called again and left another message.

This time, when he called back, he said, "Yeah, meet me at Benjamin's on Wednesday at noon. See you then."

I knew Benjamin's. It was the restaurant for a private club on Lake Washington that was very exclusive and very expensive. I'd been there several times with clients, but I thought it a really strange location to discuss selling apples at a church bazaar. I mean, lunch there would be about three hundred dollars. Couldn't we just donate that money to the church and be done with it? Plus, I hadn't been there since I'd been fired. I had been a valued customer before—how were they going to react to me now? Nothing added up, and the whole thing gave me a queasy feeling.

Benjamin's had a dress code, so I knew I had to wear a full suit to get in. I got there a little earlier than Stan. He came in with another of his clip-on ties, this time with one of the clips sticking out of his collar. He didn't have a jacket on either. Without even saying anything, the maître d' brought him a jacket and seated us.

Hmm, I thought. Things didn't add up. I was scratching my head, wondering if Stan was driving his dad's Mercedes again. Was his father a member of the club or something? *Who is this guy?*

We were seated, and everyone spoke to Stan like he owned the place. He'd definitely been there before.

Finally I couldn't take it anymore. "What is this about?" I blurted. "Why do you want me to sell apples for the bazaar?"

He laughed nervously, and his eyebrows narrowed in confusion. "What bazaar?"

"The church bazaar."

"Church bazaar?" He shook his head. "We don't sell apples for the church."

"Well," I said, probably very impatiently. "What's this all about?"

He looked timid again, but he dove in. "I was praying," he started, "and God gave me a word."

A word? I thought. *What? Like in a spelling bee?* But thankfully I didn't say that out loud. (This was the first time someone had a word from the Lord for me. I didn't even know that happened to people.)

"God told me to ask you about your employment situation," he said.

I was dumbfounded. "I just lost my job." My eyes started to fill with tears.

"That's what I thought," he went on. "God told me I'm supposed to hire you."

"Hire me?" I felt the first tear run down my cheek.

"Yes," he said. "We sell apples, mostly, and other fruit grown mostly in Washington. I need another salesman for our fruit brokerage firm."

I soon learned that Stan owned Hartmann Sales, the largest independent fruit brokerage in the state of Washington. It was a multimillion-dollar company. Perhaps it goes without saying that the car was his after all—as was the membership to Benjamin's. And to my knowledge there never was a church bazaar.

"Oh," Stan said, as if an afterthought. "How much did you make at your old job?"

I told him.

"Okay, that will be fine. Shall we order lunch?" I think my jaw dropped, and I know both my cheeks were wet by then.

As it turned out, Stan and I only lived about a mile from each other. So for the next year, Stan would pick me up at four-thirty in the morning, six mornings a week. I would drive his car, and he would read the Bible to me and ask me questions, bathing me in Scripture as a new believer. When we got to the office, we would join the rest of the team for prayer time. We had daily prayer for an hour on weekdays and two hours on Saturdays before the start of the business day.

Stan and his sales team were all longtime believers who operated their business strictly according to biblical principles. I don't just mean that they were honest and kind and forthright—though they were—but that they looked at the Scriptures as the greatest source of wisdom and knowledge available to them. As they prayed, God would give them specific instructions, and when they followed those instructions, amazing things happened. They acted according to the principles of seedtime and harvest, sowing and reaping, tithing, giving offerings, and blessing the nation of Israel. Thirty percent of the office income went into the kingdom of God, and the firstfruits of that always went to support ventures in Israel. It all seemed extremely strange to me, but I was in no position to judge, so I just listened and learned.

My initial impression as a former "big time" salesman for a prominent Seattle firm was that Stan's team was average, at best, when it came to natural sales skills. We all operated in a large brokerage room where we could hear each other's phone pitches. I had more experience in other industries and much more training—I had been an expert sales trainer at my last few positions, after all—and I understood the art of "closing the deal," so to speak. And yet in that first year of business, I did not pick up one client or sell one box of apples, while Stan and his team sold and delivered millions of dollars of fruit.

I was stupefied at those results. I would have fired me. Even in the years to come, this "average team" far exceeded anything I could do as an apple broker, regularly posting double or triple my sales. It was a terribly painful and humbling year for me, but I now thank God for that time because it taught me one of the most powerful lessons a person can learn: "And you shall remember the LORD your God, for it is He who gives you power to get wealth, that He may establish His covenant which He swore to your fathers, as it is this day" (Deuteronomy 8:18).

I am forever grateful that Stan heard from God that he was to train me up for a bigger calling. While I worked for him, my heart was being stripped of everything I thought I knew and was being taught to trust in God and God alone. It didn't take me long to see why Hartmann Sales was the number-one sales brokerage firm in Washington. They obeyed God and lived what they believed and prospered as a result. I saw it with my own eyes, heard it with my own ears, and that experience changed me—although it would take years of growing before I could walk in that truth on my own.

God didn't just give me a job with Stan so I could feed my family. He brought me into a business that knew how to operate as part of the kingdom of God. Much of what I learned there I still operate today. God was building into me for the future every step along the way.

six

ADOPTED BY THE FATHER

For you did not receive the spirit of bondage again to fear, but you received the Spirit of adoption by whom we cry out, "Abba, Father."

—ROMANS 8:15

WHEN I WAS ABOUT SIX years old, we adopted my little brother. He was delivered by our family doctor, so it was arranged that we would pick him up at the doctor's office the day after his birth. I remember it felt like we were going in for a checkup, only when we left, my sister and I had a baby brother.

In the 1950s and early 1960s, those who arranged adoptions usually tried to place children in homes where they looked as much like the rest of the family as possible. In my case this worked. My older sister and I could easily have been natural siblings. We both had olive skin, brown eyes, and brown hair just like our parents. My new little brother was a different matter—a redhead complete with pink skin, blue eyes, freckles, and a temper. It was like we'd adopted a firecracker in both looks and personality.

We didn't take him to the courthouse to finalize the adoption until he was two. We all dressed in our best clothes, piled into the car, and headed to downtown Los Angeles. We wanted to look like a happy, upstanding family because the judge was going to have to determine whether we were fit to be his family or not. My sister and I were told to be on our best behavior.

We waited in the judge's chambers until he could meet with us. I remember that my mother told me, "Now you keep an eye on him and make sure he doesn't mess up his clothes."

"All right," I said.

We waited awhile. My little brother and I were never ones to sit around too long, so he and I started playing around. We tried a game of chase, even though there wasn't much room to run around. And in the process of evading me, he ran smack dab into the corner of the judge's big oak desk. As he lay on his back, crying, I could already see the beginnings of a big black eye.

Uh-oh, I thought.

Then the eye started to swell. It was going to be one heck of a shiner. And rather than chastising me, my mother started crying. She was sure the judge was going to declare them abusive and take my little brother away from us. My dad was trying to comfort her, and I was trying really hard not to be noticed.

Then the judge burst in, and everyone tried to explain. But he waved it off almost as soon as he sat. "Boys will be boys," he said, almost laughing.

My mother smiled weakly.

They got some ice to put on my little brother's face, and then my parents and the judge dove into what seemed to be a mountain of paperwork. Mom and Dad signed everything, the judge signed everything, and then a notary came in and sealed everything.

At that moment, my little brother—as different as he looked from the rest of us—no longer belonged to his former family. He was now a Landry just like me, just like my sister, and just like my mother had become the day she married my father. Despite our different origins, on that day we were sealed into the same family.

Douglas's adoption was not merely a legal document signed and enforced but an act of covenant that changed his name and identity.

Thirty years later, in the first year I worked as a fruit broker, Stan read to me from the Scriptures every morning on the way to work, and I learned what it meant to pray for an hour or more at a time. I soon realized I was no longer the Curtis Landry I had been, part of a worldly system of wealth and excess and selfishness that wanted nothing more than to use me up and spit me out. I was switched from a society where being a Jesus freak got me fired to a place where keeping pace with everyone else around me in the pursuit of God took everything I had. For me, there was no gradual transition from the world system to the kingdom. God plucked me up out of one and threw me into the deep end of the other.

What needs to happen when we get born again is that we need to realize we have indeed become new creatures in Christ, adopted into a whole new family, sealed in a covenant relationship with our God and with our brothers and sisters in Christ. That's a wonderful thing, a big deal. But too many of us limp into Christianity as if we have our tails between our legs. Though we may not voice it or consciously recognize it, we're not quite sure being a Christian is going to be better.

One reason for this, as I have mentioned before, is because what we pass off as Christian heritage and legacy has become misshapen. So we don't step out of the world and into the covenant relationship Jesus provided for us. We don't realize He was sacrificed on the cross, rose on the third day, and then went to the right hand of the Father so He could be the advocate of that covenant. We may not even know what a covenant is supposed to be.

Even though the Bible is divided into two "testaments" (another word for covenant), we don't hear talk of "covenant" in most of our churches today. If we do, we probably think of it as an Old Testament word that doesn't have much to do with Jesus, so we miss out on so much of the richness of what it means to become part of the family of God.

What is a covenant? On the surface, it is a little like a contract—a legal agreement between two or more people or organizations. Today we sign contracts whose terms are very often lined out in page after page of legalese. When each party of the contract signs, they are saying that they will abide by what is written in those pages. The Party of the First Part is obliged to do certain things or hand over certain assets in exchange for the Party of the Second Part doing certain things or handing over certain assets.

For example, when Amazon wanted to expand their business reach to their existing customer base into organic groceries, they agreed to pay Whole Foods $13.7 billion dollars to acquire their assets and expertise. Instead of starting their own grocery business from scratch, they reached a workable agreement with Whole Foods, which had tremendous experience and expertise in the high-end natural foods grocery business. I'm sure the contract they signed to close this deal was hundreds of pages long and detailed exactly what each side could and couldn't do—in some cases creating promises that needed to be delivered upon and in others limiting liability and outlining what was not to happen. It was almost like a detailed marriage contract and probably included some kind of a "prenuptial agreement" to cover the possibility that the union might need to be dissolved down the road.

Likewise, a covenant involves an agreement and a promise to abide by it. But the main difference between a contract and a covenant is that covenants don't tend to limit responsibilities and don't have escape clauses. A covenant establishes a relationship that is intended to last. And from the beginning of time, covenants defined the kinds of relationships God developed with His people—His family on the earth.

When God instituted the sacramental covenant of marriage, for example, He never intended for divorce to be an option. The classic wedding vows reflect this:

> I, _____, take you, _____, for my lawful wife [husband], to have and to hold from this day forward, for better, for worse, for richer, for poorer, in sickness and in health, until death do us part. I will love and honor you all the days of my life.

Note that there are not any conditions or "I don't have tos" in these promises to one another. It's "everything I have I give to you" and vice versa. The responsibility built into the vows is not dependent on what the other person does or doesn't do. We're supposed to do what we vowed, regardless.

Personal covenants don't always involve marriage, however. In ancient biblical times entire families often entered into covenants together, though sometimes those would indeed be sealed by the son of one family marrying the daughter of the other. The covenant connection might be made between families that had different strengths. If you were a farmer, for instance, you might make covenant with a family of shepherd warriors who could help provide protection, wool, and milk while you covenanted to provide the other family with food from the ground.

The process of sealing the covenant might go something like

this: the heads of the two households would agree on terms that stipulated what each party promised to provide, and there would be ritual exchanges to show how each was giving themselves to the other. For instance, the two men might exchange coats to signify giving each other their authority. Think of it as a military officer exchanging his uniform jacket with a CEO's suit—the military jacket represents the officer's merits and rank, while the CEO's coat represents his wealth and position. Then they would exchange belts, because belts were where they carried their weapons; the exchange was a way of saying, "My might is for you."

Next would come a blood sacrifice and a mixing of blood, like the ritual of becoming blood brothers that used to be shown in old westerns. The household heads would cut their palms and grab each other's hand, mixing the blood of the two families. Then ash or salt would be rubbed in those wounds so they would scar. So each time that person saw the scar in the palm of his hand, he'd be reminded of his covenant partner. In a marriage covenant, similarly, a circular covenant scar would be cut around the right thumbs of the bride and groom. Today we have replaced that practice with wedding bands.

Finally, they would exchange names (this is the origin of hyphenated names in nobility that you sometimes still see today), make vows, share a covenant meal together, and then create some kind of a memorial in a place easily accessed by the two families so that each would be reminded of the covenant when going to visit the other. *Remember* is a very important covenant word. Each covenant partner should be constantly reminded to think of the welfare of the other partner and his kin.

Once a covenant was made, the partners would call each other "friend," but the bond of friendship they were speaking of was much deeper than what we think of as friendship today. This friendship was deeper even than natural family ties.

We see this same idea reflected in Jesus' words recorded by Mark:

> Then His brothers and His mother came, and standing outside they sent to Him, calling Him. And a multitude was sitting around Him; and they said to Him, "Look, Your mother and Your brothers are outside seeking You."
>
> But He answered them, saying, "Who is My mother, or My brothers?" And He looked around in a circle at those who sat about Him, and said, "Here are My mother and My brothers! For whoever does the will of God is My brother and My sister and mother. (Mark 3:31–35)

Jesus wasn't being disrespectful to His family or tossing them aside, as we see later when Jesus arranged for His mother's care at the cross (John 19:26–27) and when at least two of Jesus' younger brothers, James and Jude, became important leaders in the church. He was saying, "Whoever steps into covenant with God by doing His will, that person is in covenant with Me, and our bonds are even stronger than My bonds with My natural family."

Jesus went even further to call the disciples His friends on the night He was betrayed:

> Greater love has no one than this, than to lay down one's life for his friends. You are My friends if you do whatever I command you. No longer do I call you servants, for a servant does not know what his master is doing; but I have called you friends, for all things that I heard from My Father I have made known to you. (John 15:13–15)

In fact, all throughout their Last Supper together on that Passover evening, Jesus used covenant language and proclaimed the terms of the new covenant that would be sealed with His blood. We recall this covenant every time we take communion:

> And He took bread, gave thanks and broke it, and gave it to them, saying, "This is My body which is given for you; do this in remembrance of Me."
>
> Likewise He also took the cup after supper, saying, "This cup is the new covenant in My blood, which is shed for you." (Luke 22:19–20)

"Do this in remembrance of me"—that's covenant talk. Jesus was saying that when we take the cup at communion, we do so to be reminded of our covenant with God, the covenant that was sealed by the shedding of His blood and the giving of His body. (And there's an even deeper meaning to this that we'll look at later.)

The problem is that we as a church have forgotten almost all that covenant means. Yes, it certainly means that in Christ we have been washed of our sins and born again of the Spirit and that we have the promise of heaven. But this new covenant, which Jesus sealed by His death, burial, and resurrection, has wider, more glorious dimensions:

> You [Jesus] have redeemed us to God by Your blood
> Out of every tribe and tongue and people and nation,
> And have made us kings and priests to our God;
> And we shall reign on the earth.
>
> (REVELATION 5:9–10)

And just as important, this beautiful new covenant is a fulfillment of a series of earlier covenants between God and people. Centuries ago, the church let awareness of these covenants be washed away with the heritage that was everywhere in the early church and is practically nowhere in churches of today. We've been cut off from those covenantal roots. It's time for us to recognize that and reclaim them.

There are several examples of covenant in the Bible, but probably the most significant besides the new covenant is the one God made with Abraham and his offspring in the book of Genesis:

> Then [God] said to him, "I am the LORD, who brought you out of Ur of the Chaldeans, to give you this land to inherit it."
>
> And [Abraham] said, "Lord GOD, how shall I know that I will inherit it?" So He said to him, "Bring Me a three-year-old heifer, a three-year-old female goat, a three-year-old ram, a turtledove, and a young pigeon." Then he brought all these to Him and cut them in two, down the middle, and placed each piece opposite the other; but he did not cut the birds in two. And when the vultures came down on the carcasses, Abram drove them away. . . .
>
> And it came to pass, when the sun went down and it was dark, that behold, there appeared a smoking oven and a burning torch that passed between those pieces. On the same day the LORD made a covenant with Abram, saying: "To your descendants I have given this land, from the river of Egypt to the great river, the River Euphrates." (Genesis 15:7–11, 17–18)

While you need to look throughout the book of Genesis to see all the components of God's covenant with Abraham, it is in this passage that we see God seal it with the blood of the heifer, goat, and ram. Abraham, or Abram as he was still known at this time, had followed God's instructions and sacrificed these animals by cutting them in half and laying their halves out with their blood spilling into the middle. The point of this ceremony was to create a spectacle that would not easily be forgotten.

After he had sacrificed the animals, Abram had to wait and protect the sacrifices from predators. Then, that evening, God came in fiery form and walked between the sacrifices, consuming them. That certainly would have painted a mental image that no one was soon to forget. After that God gave Abram a promise about the land he would inherit. And God never forsook this covenant, because the same territory is where the modern nation of Israel is located today (although currently only occupying part of the promise).

As we just discussed, the animal sacrifice and the promise of land was just one piece of God's covenant with Abraham. The entire covenant unfolds piece by piece throughout Abraham's story in Genesis. Here are some of its main components:

1. God calls Abram and sets out the first tenets of His covenant with him:

> Get out of your country,
> From your family
> And from your father's house,
> To a land that I will show you.
> I will make you a great nation;
> I will bless you
> And make your name great;
> And you shall be a blessing.
> I will bless those who bless you,
> And I will curse him who curses you;
> And in you all the families of the earth shall
> be blessed.
>
> (Genesis 12:1–3)

2. God blesses Abram financially and gives him further details

about the land he would inherit and the kind of people his descendants would become:

> Abram was very rich in livestock, in silver, and in gold. (Genesis 13:2)
>
> Lift your eyes now and look from the place where you are—northward, southward, eastward, and westward; for all the land which you see I give to you and your descendants forever. And I will make your descendants as the dust of the earth; so that if a man could number the dust of the earth, then your descendants also could be numbered. Arise, walk in the land through its length and its width, for I give it to you. (Genesis 13:14–17)

3. Abram tithes back to God:

> Then Melchizedek king of Salem brought out bread and wine [elements of a covenant meal]; he was the priest of God Most High. And he blessed him [Abram] and said:
>
> "Blessed be Abram of God Most High,
> Possessor of heaven and earth;
> And blessed be God Most High,
> Who has delivered your enemies into your
>   hand."
> And he gave him a tithe of all.
>   (Genesis 14:18–20)

4. Abram sacrifices the heifer, goat, and ram and God walks

through them in their blood to ratify the covenant (Genesis
15:14–15, quoted above).

5. God gives Abram a new covenant name:

> As for Me, behold, My covenant is with you,
> and you shall be a father of many nations.
> No longer shall your name be called Abram,
> but your name shall be Abraham; for I have
> made you a father of many nations. (Genesis
> 17:4–5)

6. God declares that His covenant with Abraham and his
descendants will be everlasting:

> And I will establish My covenant between
> Me and you and your descendants after you
> in their generations, for an everlasting cove-
> nant, to be God to you and your descendants
> after you. Also I give to you and your descen-
> dants after you the land in which you are a
> stranger, all the land of Canaan, as an ever-
> lasting possession; and I will be their God.
> (Genesis 17:7–8)

7. God establishes that the "scar" of their covenant will be
circumcision—a covenant scar that will not be evident to
others. (God's people will have to walk with their inheritance as a hidden thing):

> This is My covenant which you shall keep,
> between Me and you and your descendants

after you: Every male child among you shall
be circumcised; and you shall be circumcised
in the flesh of your foreskins, and it shall be
a sign of the covenant between Me and you.
(Genesis 17:10–11)

8. God changes the name of Abraham's wife from Sarai to
Sarah and gives the promise of a future son:

As for Sarai your wife, you shall not call her
name Sarai, but Sarah shall be her name. And
I will bless her and also give you a son by her;
then I will bless her, and she shall be a mother
of nations; kings of peoples shall be from her.
(Genesis 17:15–16)

9. God refuses to keep His covenant partner out of the loop
on what His plans are:

Shall I hide from Abraham what I am doing,
since Abraham shall surely become a great
and mighty nation, and all the nations of
the earth shall be blessed in him? (Genesis
18:17–18)

10. God recognizes Abraham's authority to intercede with
Him as a representative of the earth:

The LORD said, "Because the outcry against
Sodom and Gomorrah is great, and because
their sin is very grave, I will go down now
and see whether they have done altogether

according the outcry against it that has come
to Me; and if not, I will know." . . .

Abraham still stood before the LORD.
And Abraham came near and said, "Would
You also destroy the righteous with the
wicked?" . . . Far be it from You to do such
a thing as this. . . . Shall not the Judge of all
the earth do right?" So the LORD said, "If I
find in Sodom fifty righteous within the city,
then I will spare all the place for their sakes."
(Genesis 18:20–23, 25–26)

11. Abraham ratifies that his side of the covenant—his "right
standing" with God—would be sealed through obedience and faith by being willing to offer up Isaac, and God
makes the promise of blessing the earth through the seed
of Abraham:

By Myself I have sworn, says the LORD,
because you have done this thing, and have
not withheld your son, your only son—
blessing I will bless you, and multiplying I
will multiply your descendants as the stars
of the heaven and as the sand which is on the
seashore; and your descendants shall possess the gate of their enemies. In your seed
all the nations of the earth shall be blessed,
because you have obeyed My voice. (Genesis
22:16–18)

It is interesting that the man God first made covenant with on
the earth was a man whose name, *Abram,* meant "exalted father."

Also, when God changed Abram's name, He didn't change that root. Abram become Abraham, which means "father of a multitude" (Genesis 17:5 esv, note b). From the very beginning, in other words, God had family in mind as a defining characteristic of His people. His plan was that one generation would pass the covenant down to the next—that the parents' ceiling would be their children's floor and that covenant heritage would be the foundation upon which the kingdom of God would be built.

God's covenants always filter through family, and recognizing this is one of the keys to developing a healthy relationship with our Father. A biblically cultured family is one that lives in synergy with God's ways, God's calendar, and God's culture. Its members reap the blessings of restored relationships, physical health, and financial prosperity. But to live this way today means repairing that which has been broken or buried in history, and that in turn means taking an honest and transparent look at how it became broken in the first place. We have to return to the beginning and reclaim the covenants that have been forgotten.

Biblical covenants are agreements between God and His people. God as a good Father makes covenant agreements with His people, usually patterned after the understanding that we do the small thing and God does the big thing. In other words, both sides have responsibilities to fulfill, but God carries the greater responsibility of the outcome or manifestation of the covenant.

Our covenant responsibility as His people usually involves certain conduct, heart attitudes, and choices of how we handle our time and finances—acts done in faith and obedience, just as Abraham's actions were. Enjoying the blessings of the covenant are contingent on doing these "small things" that are required of us.

This is something Stan and the others I was working with selling fruit understood. They understood the importance of a blanket faith toward God, a general sense that they were for Him and He was for them and that "all things work together for good to those who love God, to those who are the called according to His purpose" (Romans 8:28). But they also understood the power of *specific* faith: obedience to the principles laid out in Scripture; things such as the principles of seedtime and harvest, sowing and reaping, tithing, giving offerings, and blessing Israel as I mentioned before.

This is not legalism or "works before faith." It is not treating God as some kind of supernatural vending machine we feed our good deeds into and then get what we want. That kind of thinking doesn't understand covenant relationship at all.

Covenant is based on an attitude of "my all for you" from both sides. Our covenant responsibilities are not legalistic requirements but simply part of being in a covenant relationship with God. We do the small things that please Him, and He responds out of His lavish, taking-care-of-the-big-things nature as a loving Father. We bless God with our obedience and faith, and that brings us into alignment under an open heaven—it connects us more powerfully to Him. And when that happens, God has free rein to love His kids any way that He wants.

It's not a Western cause-and-effect relationship—we don't cause or obligate God to bless us by our faith and obedience. But He is true to His Word and promises. When we act according to His will, we can expect better things to happen, because, as we have seen, "He is a rewarder of those who diligently seek Him" (Hebrews 11:6). Defeat and failure, on the other hand, are the result of not knowing, understanding, or believing in our spiritual identity, which is rooted in our covenant-based, family relationship with God.

I believe that it is time for the church to return and rebuild our spiritual foundations and heritage with power and dominion as is promised in God's covenants. This recovery process starts with each of us walking in a victorious identity as a covenant daughter or son and as a spiritual king and priest, not as one who is begging at the gate defeated and powerless.

The majority of people obtain their views of what Christianity is like and who God is from observing the Christian community. And too often we Christians do not ground our lives in the Bible or have a full understanding of what God has called us to and promised us. Instead, we look to our neighbors and our leaders for how to live. That's quite normal, but it only works in a positive way when we recognize our God-provided heritage and walk in our true identities. No wonder we're confused about who we are and what we're about. So few around us are walking in the fullness God wants for us.

We need to realize that, in the same way my brother became a Landry when his official papers were signed and notarized, we became God's children when He signed, sealed, and delivered our adoption papers into His kingdom family,

> having predestined us to adoption as sons by Jesus Christ to Himself, according to the good pleasure of His will . . .
>
> In Him we have redemption through His blood, the forgiveness of sins, according to the riches of His grace, which He made to abound toward us in all wisdom and prudence. . . .
>
> In whom also, having believed, you were sealed with the Holy Spirit of promise, who is the guarantee of our inheritance until the redemption of the purchased possession, to the praise of His glory. (Ephesians 1:5, 7–8, 13–14)

It's time to recognize and re-embrace that covenant.

seven

ACCIDENTALLY
JEWISH

For this is the covenant that I will make with the house of Israel after those days, says the LORD: I will put My laws in their mind and write them on their hearts; and I will be their God, and they shall be My people.

—HEBREWS 8:10

SHORTLY AFTER I GOT SAVED, I was invited to be the best man in a messianic Jewish[1] wedding. Before attending the wedding, the groom suggested I attend a Friday *Shabbat*[2] service to get a feel for the congregation and the way services were conducted. It would be my first real experience of both "messianic" and "Jewish."

I was very uncomfortable at first because the service was

unlike any I had been to in a church. For one thing, the praise and worship songs were all in Hebrew. But as the music began and the voices started to join in chorus, I found myself overwhelmed. My eyes began to burn and tears began to roll down my cheeks. I didn't understand a single word, but those songs touched me to my very soul.

The service continued with songs, readings, and prayers. Everything about it was completely foreign to me, and yet there was something strangely familiar and comforting to my soul. This was something I had never experienced before. Something about it transcended mental understanding—deep within me, my soul was reacting to what I was experiencing.

I felt like God was saying, "Welcome home."

At that time, as far as I knew, my only connection to Judaism was the fact that my adoptive mother was a nonreligious, nonpracticing Jew. I'd had almost no connection to Jewish faith or culture while growing up. And yet I had repeatedly been mistaken for being Jewish as a kid and had often found myself identifying with Jewish people.

There was Sandy Koufax, for example. I'd never been much of a baseball player overall, but I could throw hard and accurately, so I'd pitched in Little League. For a young pitcher in early 1960s Los Angeles, there was no way Koufax was not going to be a hero—and of course he was Jewish.

And there were a lot of Jewish families in our neighborhood. There were even a fair number of Jewish kids in my Catholic school because it was the best school in the zip code. So a lot of my friends were Jewish, and that seemed perfectly normal to me. I didn't see anything different or special about them. They were just kids I knew.

I remember trying to decide which Boy Scout troop I wanted to join. I had been part of a Cub Scout pack near my home, not the one at the Catholic school, so when I was old enough for Boy Scouts, I had a choice between the troop at St. Jerome's, a Catholic one, or a Jewish one that also met nearby. My parents said the choice was up to me. So I set up visits with each troop.

The guys in the Jewish troop said, "Okay, this is what we do. We hike the John Muir Trail every year. We do three hikes to build up to it, and then we hike a fifty-mile section of the trail. We're going to hike Mount Whitney this fall. Then we have these campouts . . ." and on and on they went. I'm an outdoors person, so all of that sounded great.

My visit to the Catholic troop was completely different. They said, "Well, we'd like to do this, and we hope to do that, but we don't have any money, so who knows. We have these fund-raisers planned, and if we can raise enough, we might do this or that."

To me the choice was clear. *Those guys are planning hikes and outings, while these guys are planning fund-raisers. I'm going with the hikes and camping!* So I decided to join the Jewish troop.

My parents were totally supportive, but they also knew there could be risks I had no clue about. So before I made the final call, my dad and mom sat me down.

"Curtis, we need to talk to you."

"Sure."

"This troop you're joining, it's mostly made up of Jewish kids."

"Yeah, I know."

"Like the Johnsons and the Barons next door."

"Yeah."

My dad took a breath. "Well, you may experience people treating you differently when you are with these kids. Some people are prejudiced. There are people who just don't like Jewish people, and sometimes they're mean to them."

"All right," I said. I had no clue as to what he was talking about.

So I joined the Jewish troop and had a great time at the meetings. We hiked, we made stuff, we worked on our badges, and we got our rewards and rankings. Even though I was only eleven and they didn't usually let the youngest guys go on all the hikes, I went on them all after doing the work to prove I wouldn't slow anyone down. It was great. I loved it. I was making friends and having a great time.

Then, that summer, we went on our first Boy Scout jamboree. We set up our tents, built fires, and participated in the activities with the other troops that were there. We were having a great time. Then came Sunday morning.

Faith is a very important part of Boy Scouts, so everyone went to the nondenominational service that morning—everyone except us, of course. Jews have their services on Saturday to honor *Shabbat*, so no one in our troop even thought to go to the Sunday morning church service. Instead, we went down to the river and skipped rocks and goofed around.

We were just having a good time. Then, all of a sudden, two or three rocks came flying from the top of the hill and hit the ground around us. We looked up and saw a bunch of guys standing up on the ridge. "Hey you, kikes," one of them yelled and then started another volley of rocks.

I remember thinking, *What's a kike?* Then I started thinking about what to do next.

When I was in grade school, my dad had sat me down and told me, "If I ever hear of you starting a fight, you're going to get it from me when you get home." I nodded that I understood. Then he went on, "But if I ever hear of you walking away from a fight you didn't start, you're going to hear it from me when you get home as well." Being a former marine and a boxer, he wasn't going to have any kids who couldn't defend themselves. He taught us all to box, even my sister. We'd be in the living room with the big gloves on, swinging at each other. He'd sound a bell just like in a regular ring. We had our corners, Coke bottles with water in them for between rounds, and even a spit bucket, the whole deal.

Well, this wasn't a fight I had started, so I knew it wasn't one I could walk away from. "All right, guys," I said. "Get some rocks."

We started returning fire, and my pitching skills won the day. I was pelting guys and the battle was soon over. We were lucky no one got seriously hurt. But of course we got in serious trouble. I and a couple of others got sent home early.

My dad picked me up and wasn't too pleased. When I told him what had happened, he seemed to understand a little, but warned me of the danger of throwing rocks. "You fight with your fists, not weapons," he told me. "They're just other kids. You don't want to kill them."

I nodded, and we rode for a while in silence.

Then, the gears turning in my head, I asked, "Dad, what's a kike?" He looked at me sideways and seemed to take in what had happened with a deeper understanding. "That's one of those names we never call people," he said. "Never use that word again."

I didn't understand, but I knew when not to push him any further as well, so I dropped it. That was the first brush I had with anti-Semitism, and it wouldn't be the last.

When I got into high school, I dated a couple of Jewish girls and didn't think anything of it. At one point I was in a pretty serious relationship with the girl whose mother told me I wasn't remedial, so I used to hang out with her and her other Jewish friends all the time.

That was in the early 1970s, when the Jesus Movement was sweeping California. The Jesus freaks at our school liked to gather in circles during lunch. Someone always had a guitar, and they'd sing Jesus songs. Everyone at school was long-haired and hippied-out back then, and it seemed like everyone was either a Jesus freak or smoking pot. And of course we had police around all the time because there had been riots in downtown Los Angeles. So my friends and I thought it was easier to just keep to ourselves.

One day, out of the blue, one of the Jesus kids left his circle and came over to the table where we were eating lunch. He sat down and tried to start a conversation about Jesus, but none of us was interested. I just thought he was weird. "Why the heck do you do all this Jesus stuff?" I asked him. "Why are you so obsessed?"

"Well, we're Christians now," he told me, "and we believe in Jesus." I didn't think that was much of an answer, but I could tell he wasn't done yet. "But *your* people," he said, pointing at me, "you guys killed Jesus." Then, as if coming to some kind of a conclusion, "I guess that's why He's not for you. He's only for us." Then he got up and left.

I was shocked. I'd never heard anything like that before, and I hadn't even gotten a chance to tell him I wasn't Catholic or Jewish, though I didn't really know what being Catholic meant either. It just seemed so strange for him to say something like that. I'd never killed anyone and neither had my friends.

"Whatever," I said to his retreating back. But his words still wounded me. From that moment on, because he had been so hateful, I wanted nothing to do with those Jesus freaks.

In the years after that, there were several other occasions when people assumed I was Jewish. I had always just shrugged it off— until that *Shabbat* service in Washington, when I heard Hebrew for the first time. It felt like a clarion call, but to what, I didn't know.

————

Grace Church and the guys I worked with were filled with concern about Israel and about the Jews returning to their homeland. I'd never really thought about the nation of Israel up until then.

But now it seemed like I was hearing about it all the time. I remember being part of a men's prayer meeting—there were ten or twelve guys there—and one of the leaders said he had a Scripture to "pray into." He opened his Bible and read Isaiah 60:8–9:

> Who are these who fly like a cloud,
> And like doves to their roosts?
> Surely the coastlands shall wait for Me;
> And the ships of Tarshish will come first,
> To bring your sons from afar,
> Their silver and their gold with them,
> To the name of the LORD your God,
> And to the Holy One of Israel,
> Because He has glorified you.

After we prayed about it for a while, the leader shared his belief that the only thing Isaiah could be referring to when he said, "Who are these who fly like a cloud?" was 747s. His comment dumbfounded me on a number of levels. I thought, *How would some guy from thousands of years ago know about 747s?* But others around me were nodding. Men started to bow their heads and pray. Here and there different people spoke out impressions they were getting. Men started to pray out loud for Israel and about the return of "sons from afar."

We continued to pray like that for several weeks. And then at one of the meetings, the man who had said the thing about 747s stood to say that he believed we were supposed to hire 747s to go to Russia and former Soviet States and help Jews who were trapped there get to Israel. (This was in the 1990s, remember, so the Soviet Union had only recently collapsed.) In response, many started to pray again and some spoke out what they were sensing, agreeing with what he had said. It was amazing.

After several weeks of continued prayer, the consensus was

that it was indeed time for the Jewish people who were in the former Soviet Union to make *aliyah*—to leave where they were and immigrate to Israel. (In Hebrew *aliyah* is the term used to describe the Jews' return to their homeland and is translated as "ascent.") Confirming this, some in our group read Isaiah 60:4–5:

> Lift up your eyes all around, and see:
> They all gather together, they come to you;
> Your sons shall come from afar,
> And your daughters shall be nursed at your side.
> Then you shall see and become radiant,
> And your heart shall swell with joy;
> Because the abundance of the sea shall be turned to you,
> The wealth of the Gentiles shall come to you.

I'd never imagined that God could use ancient Scriptures to speak to modern people in a way that gave such specific instruction. It made my head spin. But everyone around me was in agreement. We began writing checks to help lease the aircraft. The wealth of us Gentiles was going to finance the return of Jews to the promised land, their *aliyah*.

In the days to come, Christie and I would actually witness leased 747s leaving Boeing Field in Seattle to fly to Russia, pick up Jews, and fly them to the land of their fathers like "doves to their roost." It was an incredible experience, and we felt the presence of God in everything that we did concerning this venture, which was our first major endeavor focused on blessing Israel.

Within our circles, this effort became known as Operation Exodus. As it unfolded, we realized that the two bags people were allowed to bring with them on the planes would only carry so much. Those immigrating would have to leave most of their family heirlooms and treasures behind.

When we talked about this, someone pointed to the ships
mentioned in Isaiah 60:9:

> And the ships of Tarshish will come first,
> To bring your sons from afar,
> Their silver and their gold with them.

We prayed into that, and then someone in the group reached
out to a ship broker in Cyprus who said he could provide us with
a ship that would allow the immigrants, mostly elderly, to bring
more of their personal belongings. We agreed to lease a ship in
Cyprus and sent two men over with a briefcase full of cash to
handle the financial transaction. When they arrived, however,
the broker told them that the payment was two weeks late; he had
given our ship to someone else. The next available ship was not in
Cyprus but in the Tarshish region.

You can imagine how hearing that affected us. God was fulfilling the word He'd sent to us *to the letter*.

These experiences would prove foundational for Christie
and me. They opened to us the miraculous ways that God can
move when His people come together to pray, listen for what He
is saying, and then act according to His words—not rashly, but
in ongoing prayer and intercession. With all that was happening
around me, between the guys at work and how they operated and
the mountain-moving faith we experienced at church, I felt like
I'd been thrust into the middle of the book of Acts. God seemed to
be fast-tracking us, maybe because He had big things He wanted
us to do.

One of the keys to successful Christian living is understanding that God is the same yesterday, today, and forever. Regardless,
of whether you are Jew or Gentile, God will never leave you nor
forsake you, and He "is not a man that He should lie" (Numbers

23:19). He is faithful to fulfill His Word—and I was beginning to see this with my own eyes.

Things were moving so fast around us, it was hard to imagine God had anything else up His sleeve, anything that could move things along any more profoundly. That only goes to show you how small our imaginations can be. Because as I was soon to learn, all of this had only been a setup for what would turn out to be the biggest turning point of my life.

eight

FINDING MY FATHER— AND MYSELF

Bring out the best robe and put it on him, and put a
ring on his hand and sandals on his feet. And bring
the fatted calf here and kill it, and let us eat and be
merry; for this my son was dead and is alive again;
he was lost and is found.

—LUKE 15:22–24

BY THE SUMMER OF 1993, Christie, Megann, and I had moved to the east side of the Cascades, closer to the orchards that grew the fruit for which I was a broker. We now lived in the bustling little town of Wenatchee, Washington, in a beautiful home overlooking the Columbia River, where it cut through the middle of the state traveling south toward Oregon. By now I was driving myself to work for our early-morning prayer meetings and was beginning to get the hang of selling "by the Spirit" rather than by the old methods I'd used in the insurance business. But one morning as I climbed out of bed, I felt an unusual prompting to stay home and pray instead of going in to pray with my business partners.

I called in to let Stan know, and he said it would be fine. Then I went into my home office and began to pray.

No one else in the house was awake at that hour, so I knelt in complete silence. It was extremely quiet outside; no wind was blowing or trees rustling, which was unusual for our home perched high on a hill. I felt such a strong presence of the Lord that I was soon lying facedown. It felt almost like a weight was pressing on my back and pushing my body against the hard floor. My spirit felt excitement, anticipation, and even a touch of what you might call godly anxiety. I sensed something extremely important was coming.

I lay there in wait. I lay there expecting. Since the last major word I'd received from the Lord was about transporting Jews back to Israel, I thought God might have a similar task for me this time as well. So I was completely caught off guard when I heard the Lord whisper, *"I want to reconnect you to your biological father."*

What?

I was so shocked that my body literally began to tremble. I had never asked God about my biological parents and never had a serious thought about finding them. As far as I was concerned, Ray and Rita Landry were my parents. I had no "missing pieces" from my childhood that finding my biological parents would fill in. Or so I thought.

At the same time, my mind raced through all the various scenarios that discovering my natural father could involve, and I confess that although some were good, most were very negative.

What if he is in prison?

What if he doesn't want to talk to me?

What if he's dead?

My mind ran wild. "Lord," I prayed, "are you really sure you want me to open this can of worms?"

Then I heard in my heart as clearly as if it had been an audible voice, *"When I open a can of worms, I take care of all the worms."*

In that moment the peace of the Lord fell on me. My mind was suddenly clear of all the possible disasters finding my father could cause, and I began to wonder about how I would begin to start looking for him.

I knew, though, that if God was telling me to start this quest, it wasn't so He could laugh at me when I failed. He was going to "take care of all the worms," after all. And if He was asking me to do something that wasn't born out of my own desires, then He had a reason.

Still, I was resistant. I didn't do anything about it that day, and when I finished my prayer time, I went to work.

The following day I felt compelled to stay home again. As I prayed in my home office this time, God began to outline the steps I should take to find my father. And this time I surrendered to His will.

You have to remember that this was still in the 1990s, so it wasn't as if I could just Google my biological dad's name or find his Facebook page or something like that. The first step God gave me was to call information in Los Angeles and ask for the number to Los Angeles Adoption Agency Services. He wanted me to take the morning off work and call that same day.

So I did. I called information and asked for the number to Los Angeles Adoption Agency Services.

"I don't have a number for anything by that name," the operator told me. I breathed a sigh of relief. I was off the hook. Then, before I'd even had a chance to thank her for her time, she said, "This is the number you need." She rattled off the digits and I wrote them down.

It wasn't until after we'd hung up that I realized how strange that conversation had been. It wasn't her job to look for things that she wasn't specifically asked for. What were the odds that I would get just the right operator who would know just the right number that I needed to call without my even pressing her for it? I began to feel that God really was at work.

But I hadn't seen anything yet.

As my fingers began dialing the number the operator had provided, I felt anxiety building with each button I pressed. Apparently the number bypassed the information line and went straight to the desk of a woman in the Los Angeles County records department.

"This is Martha,"[1] she answered.

I fumbled through my request. This was my name, I was born May 11, 1955, somewhere in Los Angeles, in a Catholic hospital. I wanted to find out about my biological father.

"I'm sorry, sir," she said. "These records are sealed. I can't give out that kind of information."

She sounded like an older woman. I instantly pictured a strict, no-nonsense nun like the ones at my parochial school. There was no way she was going to break the rules for me. Again, I thought I was off the hook.

But then she asked, "Young man, may I ask you why you are looking for your biological parents?"

I thought, *What the heck. This is all or nothing.* So I told her the whole story. It was God's thing anyway, so why would I hide that He was the one who told me to call? He was going to take care of all the worms, right?

I was sure she was going to think that I was some kind of

a religious fanatic. To make matters worse, my voice started cracking as tears threatened to flow. My words came in gulps and emotion overtook me. I wasn't sure I could finish. But I did. And then there was a moment of silence on the other end of the line.

The woman lowered her voice as if she didn't want anyone in the office around her to hear. "Here's who you need to call. She's a private detective who specializes in this kind of stuff." She recited the number as if from memory. "Please do not tell anyone that you got it from me."

I said I wouldn't tell a soul.

"I will be praying for you," she said, then hung up.

I sat there, stunned. It appeared that God had people everywhere. Slowly I put down the receiver, feeling emotionally exhausted. The heaviness of the Spirit of God and the emotional outpouring left me feeling like I needed to lie down, yet it was still morning and I had only made two phone calls.

I went to the kitchen and poured myself another cup of coffee, hoping the caffeine would give me the energy I needed to call the private investigator. Then I went upstairs to talk to Christie. I shared what had happened that morning—the amazing grace I had experienced thus far—and told her about the call I would make next. Together we prayed and agreed that the Lord would open all the correct doors and that the enemy would not be able to send any counterfeits to delay or hinder the process. Then I returned to my office. I prayed again briefly, gathered up my strength, and once more pressed the numbers I'd been given into the phone.

"Hello," a woman answered.

"Hello," I answered back. "My name is Curtis Landry."

"How can I help you, Mr. Landry?"

"I'm looking for my biological father."

There was a moment of silence on the other end of the phone. "How did you get my number?"

"She asked me not to say."

I could sense her nodding on the other end of the line. Then she launched straight into her fee structure and what I could expect from her services. It sounded like she didn't want me to get my hopes up. She definitely wanted me to know I was paying for her time, not for a particular result. She was very detailed and appeared to know her stuff.

"You need to be patient, Mr. Landry. These things take time, and I can make no promises for getting you the answers you want. Something like this can take years, and even at the end of a search we often know little more than we did at the beginning."

I agreed to her terms. I was committed, but I also knew this was not the same kind of woman as Martha at the records office. She was a tough businesswoman and was not going to end the call with "I'll be praying for you."

She started walking me through a list of personal background questions. What was my full name? What was the date of my birth? Did I know the name of the hospital? The questions went on and on. I answered each one as best as I could.

"Um, excuse me for a minute." The phone clunked as she laid the receiver down on her desk, and then I heard the sound of papers shuffling and a door creaking open. I surmised that someone had just come in, because I heard another voice ask, "What are you working on?"

The PI answered, "I'm on the phone with a Curtis Landry, and he's looking for his biological family."

"Curtis Landry?"

"Yes."

"I have a Curtis Landry file right here," I heard the other woman say.

I heard footsteps, then more shuffling.

The PI picked up the phone and said, "Oh my God." More

shuffling. "In forty years, I never had anything like this happen. I . . . I have your file right here on my desk. It was just now delivered." Neither of us could believe it, especially when she explained what was going on.

First of all, this was a sealed state file. Files like that were extremely hard to get access to. And what were the odds that the other woman would walk in with my file under her arm at the exact moment the PI was on the phone with me? That my file, with my original birth certificate in it, was the file being exchanged to be entered into the database that day? To this day, I don't know why or how it could have happened, except that it was God.

But that wasn't all. Normally, in situations where a young mother was giving up a child for adoption, she would not have given the real name of the father. Most birth certificates under those circumstances would name the father as "John Doe." But the father listed on my birth certificate was Joseph Ambrose McCaughey, II, and I had been given the name Joseph Ambrose McCaughey, III. The PI was dumbfounded again—something I got the impression didn't happen often. Then she gave me the number of a man in the Northeast who shared my father's last name, McCaughey, and who happened to have done a lot of genealogical work as a hobby.

So I made a fourth phone call.

As things had gone all morning, the man I needed to speak with answered his phone and was glad to help. He checked his research. "The second, you said? I show a Joseph Ambrose McCaughey the second who lives in West Palm Beach, Florida." He read off the man's address and the phone number he had for him. "According to what I have here," he went on, "he was born in Pawtucket, Rhode Island."

I almost dropped the phone. My adoptive father, Ray Landry, was from Pawtucket, Rhode Island.

I thanked the man and hung up, feeling nauseated and about

to pass out. The private detective had just told me that the process of finding my biological father could take years with no positive results. I had gotten a very likely prospect in four phone calls over the span of only a few hours. What I had just experienced was impossible, but then again, "with God all things are possible" (Matthew 19:26).

But I had one more call to make—no time to lose.

I dialed. The phone rang. A man with a familiar Rhode Island accent said, "Hello?"

I swallowed. "Are you Joseph McCaughey?"

"Yes."

"Are you Joseph *Ambrose* McCaughey?"

"What are you trying to sell?" he snapped.

I panicked for an instant, thinking he was going to hang up. "I'm sorry," I said quickly. "My name is Curtis Edmond Landry. I was born on May 11, 1955, at Queen of Angels hospital in Los Angeles, and I want to know if you are my father."

There was a long pause. "What year? What month? Where?"

I repeated what I had just said. There was another pause, and this time the voice on the other end of the line was quite a bit friendlier. "Young man, I think we have something to talk about."

And talk we did.

For the next two hours he shared the events that had led up to May 11, 1955, and the reasons I was given up for adoption. He explained that I had been conceived out of wedlock while he was in the air force, stationed in Northern California. He and my mother had wanted to get married, but both families had been firmly against it. His family, the McCaugheys, were devoted Irish Catholics and they weren't about to let their son marry outside the faith.

"Outside the faith?" I asked.

"Yes," he said. "Your mother was Jewish."

My mother was Jewish!

The same kind of tears that had fallen when I heard praise and worship in Hebrew began to fill my eyes again. I had been mistaken for being Jewish time and again and always denied it. *But I had been wrong.*

If my biological mother, like my adoptive mother, was Jewish—then *I* was Jewish.

My world was about to take a whole new direction, with God fully at the helm.

nine

INTENTIONALLY
JEWISH

> *But this is the covenant that I will make with the house*
> *of Israel after those days, says the LORD: I will put My*
> *law in their minds, and write it on their hearts; and I*
> *will be their God, and they shall be My people.*
>
> —JEREMIAH 31:33

JOSEPH WENT ON TO EXPLAIN that my biological mother's family had been just as opposed to an interfaith marriage as his were. His parents wanted him to settle down with a good Irish-Catholic girl, and my mother's parents wanted her to settle down with a good Portuguese Jewish boy. There was no convincing the families otherwise. No matter how much the two of them wanted it, there was no getting married without being ostracized from both sides of the family.

They considered getting an abortion, but neither felt comfortable with the idea. They ended up going to a Catholic priest on the air force base for counseling, and he strongly recommended adoption. In order to do this, my mother would have to consent to having her baby in a Catholic hospital. She would then surrender me to the Catholic adoption agency that would oversee my adoption into, most likely, a Catholic family. All this was a huge sacrifice for her, but she preferred it to the alternative, so she agreed.

I realized she must really have been in love with Joseph. Why else would she put his name on the birth certificate and name me after him? Her last official act of having anything to do with me was one that honored my father and ultimately led me back to him. I was grateful for that on so many different levels.

After my dad and mother decided I would be surrendered to the Catholic orphanage after I was born, my dad asked to be reassigned to another air base. He couldn't take being near my mother without seeing her. So before I was born, he transferred to Bangor, Maine, where he was almost immediately involved in a serious plane crash.

He was on an air refueling plane and after a failed refueling, the pilot decided to try to land with the fuel, which was always a dangerous proposition. Heavier than usual, the plane came in hard, scraped the tarmac, and exploded in flames. My dad jumped out, and as he scrambled to get away, another crewman jumping behind him landed right in the small of his back, breaking it and paralyzing him. He lay there helpless and on fire until someone came and rescued him.

Remarkably, he survived, but with burns over 90 percent of his body. He would be in the hospital for months, unable to do anything but eat, sleep, and slowly heal. He was basically on life support and completely cut off from the world. Even if my mother had tried to contact him, he would have been unable to reply, nor did he have any way to reach out to her. Plus, he felt incredible guilt for having abandoned her and me, and he was convinced the accident was God's punishment. That made it even harder to look back.

By the time he was up and about again, he'd completely lost track of my mother. The last he'd heard she'd moved out of Northern California, but he had no idea where. They'd never been in contact again. (I would be equally unsuccessful in locating her.)

As that long phone call came to an end, I was again physically and emotionally exhausted, and even more coffee wasn't going to help. It was so much to take in. Joseph and I agreed we'd stay in touch and see each other when given the opportunity. I gave him my contact information and hung up. Then I sat there dazed, looking out over the Columbia River valley, wondering about the significance of what had just happened.

Without any prompting or curiosity about it on my part, God had asked me to find my biological father. Then, in a miraculous handful of hours—an impossibly short amount of time, in retrospect—I had gone from not caring who he was to understanding why he and my mother had given me up and why they had never looked for me. I had suddenly been reconnected to a heritage I had never dreamed I had. *I'm Jewish*. What exactly did that mean?

My mind ran through all the connections I'd had with Jewish people over the years, and I had to wonder about the coincidences, which suddenly didn't feel like coincidences at all. Then I remembered something a man at church had said to me about a year after I had my Jacuzzi conversion. He said my call as a Christian would be like that of the prophet Jeremiah. He had advised me to read the entire book from beginning to end as soon as I could, and a day or so later I had done just that. The words had come so alive to me as I read that it was almost as if I were hearing an audible voice that shook me to my very soul.

I remembered the words of Jeremiah 1:5: "Before I formed you in the womb I knew you," virtually jumping off the page at me. *In my mother's womb*, I thought. My father's words rang in my ears, telling me I had almost been aborted. The fact that God had used a Catholic priest to speak wisdom and life to my parents meant that God Himself had saved me. And His protection hadn't stopped there. My soul shaked with the revelation of how the love of God had protected me from car accidents, from motorcycle accidents, and from other dangerous and violent situations common in a large city.

The next words of the Jeremiah verse then came to mind: "Before you were born I sanctified you." Being sanctified simply means being set apart or put into a place of value or protection. *But set apart from what?* What did it mean that I was to be like Jeremiah?

"I ordained you a prophet to the nations." Those were the next words.

I felt as if my breath had been taken away. A sense of the fear of the Lord engulfed me. I was overwhelmed with what I perceived to be the responsibility of someone who speaks on behalf of God as Jeremiah did. Was that even the way God still worked today? It seemed impossible, but all the evidence was there right in front of me.

I'd had a very intense, unusual experience of being born again. Shortly after that, God had literally plucked me out of the world and dropped me into a job and lifestyle where I had very little face-to-face contact with anyone who was not a radical believer. I mean, after all, who gets on-the-job training in how to pray an hour a day and two hours on Saturday? Then I was thrust into a prayer group where Old Testament prophecy came alive and was acted on with powerful confirmation that God was directing everything right before my eyes. And not only that, the prophecy that I had seen walked out was directly connected to blessing Israel, the land of the Jewish people.

The land of *my* people.

In the first half of my life, I had drawn attention to myself through my accomplishments and my shenanigans. I had built a counterfeit identity to impress others and to make myself feel good about myself. And I had used drugs and alcohol and ego to cover up and try to hide the gaping holes in my soul. But now, as I looked back over the few short years since Jesus had visited me in my bathroom, I realized my counterfeit identity had been dying that whole time and was almost gone. I had a new purpose. I had a new identity. And now I had a new heritage. I had been called to be a witness and a voice for God's kingdom on earth. No doubt there would be a long journey of preparation, but I was on my way.

I want to stop my story here for a moment and make sure you understand some things about identity, purpose, and calling. Every good gift comes from God (James 1:17), because God is love (1 John 4:8). Your calling and purpose is one of the most precious gifts God has to give you. And your God-given purpose and destiny may or may not involve callings that are traditionally considered to be ministry.

God created each one of us for a unique and special purpose, and He put this purpose into us by putting desires in our hearts. God can give you an innate desire for a certain job, career, or position. He may birth a desire within you for a certain lifestyle or home. Your heart may be burdened for a cause or outreach.

These desires—good desires—come from God the Father, our Creator. But too often the enemy will try to quench, kill, or derail those God-given desires and dreams. He may do it through other people or groups or use circumstances to discourage you from pursuing your dreams. Or he may convince you that your

God-given desires grow out of idle thoughts, ego, or selfishness. Why? Because the devil doesn't want God's will done upon the earth, and he thinks that if he can stop God's representatives, he can stop God. The key to knowing the difference is given in Hebrews 4:12, which says that God weighs the intent of the heart, the "why" behind the desire. You have to ask yourself the why to weigh the intent. If the reason is fear or pride, that is not a God-given desire. Your desires are not things you come up with on your own; they are seeds God has planted within you to help lead you into your identity.

So many people settle for less because they perceive it to be easier; they don't want to press into God or "ask for too much." This is what kills many dreams. And it usually happens for one or more of the following three reasons:

1. *We don't know who God is.* We don't see Him as the loving Father He is, eager to pour out good things on His children for both the mission He's given them *and* for their enjoyment. Remember Hebrews 11:6 we discussed earlier? We can't please God if we don't believe that "He is a rewarder of those to diligently seek Him." It's tough to be in alignment with heaven if you believe God is some kind of stingy curmudgeon.

2. *We don't know our identities according to Scripture.* Romans 8:14 tells us, "For as many as are led by the Spirit of God, these are sons [and daughters] of God." Some Christians might insert the word *servant* into this passage, but that's not what it says. You don't "adopt" (the term used in Romans 8:15) servants; nor do servants call you Father. When we don't come to the Father knowing that we're the "King's kids," we hem and haw like we have no right to be in His presence. Once again, that puts us out of alignment.

3. *We focus on circumstances rather than who our God is.* When we let lack or hardship be bigger than God, we again "slam the door" on an open heaven. There's no faith in believing God is too small to handle what you're facing. If you accept your circumstances as insurmountable, as they say in Oklahoma, you're "hitching your horse up to the wrong wagon."

Note that each of these reasons for giving up on our dreams and desires comes from accepting a counterfeit identity—from accepting a false sense of who you are, who God has created you to be, and who you should be in relationship to Him. So in order to live into your God-given calling and destiny, you need to put that counterfeit identity to death. That can be painful, but it has to happen in order for you to become who God has called you to become.

In my case, God made the process relatively easy. Before I got born again, I was worn out. I was tired. So after I got born again and thrust into this new world of on-fire believers, I had no desire to stay connected to my old identity. The counterfeit identity, although fun at times, had given me very little lasting reward and had not provided a lasting sense of fulfillment. So I was more than ready to throw myself into the journey to find the fullness of what I was created for.

That journey begins for all of us with the dying to our distorted, counterfeit identities and surrendering to the resurrection process that is facilitated through the Holy Spirit. It is a three-step process.

1. We must forgive those who put false labels and expectations on us.
2. We must forgive God and ourselves for any past unmet desires. We must verbally renounce any negative labels, pledges, judgments, descriptions, or complaints that we or

someone else have spoken over us, such as "I am worth-less," "I'll never amount to anything," "I'll never trust anyone again," "All men [women] are alike," "All pastors are the same," or "I am just like my mother [or father, grandparent, uncle, aunt]." Anything we have spoken over ourselves that puts us down or holds us back needs to be renounced. We must come out of agreement with anything that says we are less than.

3. We must also cut off any soul ties that keep us connected to the false identity such statements reflect.

What is a soul tie? It's my term for the most dynamic entry point for the enemy to speak into our minds to trick and manipulate. It is a physical or emotional attachment that drags us down, makes us codependent, or impedes our success. It can be to a person, a place, an object, or a circumstance. Sometimes, for instance, people identify so much with a sickness that it becomes part of their perceived identity—a soul tie. Mental illness and emotional disorders are often associated with or magnified by soul ties. Soul ties can be generational as well as personal. We carry on attachments that began with our parents or grandparents or even further back.

When we filter decisions through unhealthy soul ties, we typically end up making bad choices based on fear, distress, or drama. We repeat dysfunctional patterns that hold us back from blessing and success. We make emotionally charged decisions that can result in tragedy, and we ultimately hurt ourselves and those surrounding us—especially those who care the most about us. It is important that we identify these areas in our lives and do whatever we must to cut ourselves off from them.

Since we are surrounded by so great a cloud of witnesses, *let us lay aside every weight*, and the sin which so easily ensnares us, and

let us run with endurance the race that is set before us, looking
unto Jesus, the author and finisher of our faith. (Hebrews 12:1–2,
emphasis added)

We can battle against these attachments when we renew our
minds by looking into the mirror of Scripture, discovering who
we really are by doing the things it says, and grabbing hold of its
promises.

For if anyone is a hearer of the word and not a doer, he is like
a man observing his natural face in a mirror; for he observes
himself, goes away, and immediately forgets what kind of man
he was. But he who looks into the perfect law of liberty and
continues in it, and is not a forgetful hearer but a doer of the
work, this one will be blessed in what he does. (James 1:23–25)

It is especially effective to apply Scriptures that speak to the
particular attachment we are challenged with, whether it involves a
spouse, a child, an area of finance, a health threat, or something else.

In order to break a soul tie, we must first acknowledge that it
exists. Denial simply acts as camouflage and causes confusion. It
keeps us identified with the area of sin and attachment as a friend
instead of a foe. The excuse often sounds something like, "Well,
that's just who I am," or "I was born this way." We make excuses
that keep us in agreement with things that are holding us back.
And all too often we can't even see what we're doing, which is
why prayer, meditation on Scripture, and seeking wise counsel
are important. It may take a while, but if we ask our heavenly
Father to reveal these areas of unhealthy attachment, He will
eventually get through to us.

Once we have recognized a soul tie in our lives, we must treat
it like any other sin: we must confess and repent. And make no

mistake—these unhealthy attachments are sinful because they get in the way of what God is wanting to do in our lives and hinders obedience. (It's the disobedience and rebellion that is the root of sin.) But when we confess and repent, God is faithful and just to forgive and restore, and we must receive His forgiveness.

Finally, we must do some forgiving on our own so that we can move ahead freely. We must forgive ourselves and others for any part played in opening doors that allowed soul ties to come or thrive. And we must forgive former partners or abusers who took advantage of the soul ties in our lives that further exacerbated our counterfeit identities.

After I was born again and connected to my biological roots, it took years for me to make peace in my soul with the constant nagging burden of the years I had wasted being "somebody else" and striving to be someone I was never meant to be. I had trouble accepting God's forgiveness for this and forgiving myself as well. What helped me was realizing that in some ways I was like the prodigal son in the Bible (Luke 15:11–32). No, I hadn't blatantly rebelled against my Father and run away the way the prodigal son did. But I still felt I had lived the majority of my life in a pigpen, so to speak, wasting His gifts and squandering an inheritance I didn't even know I had.

What helped me come to terms with those "lost" years was realizing how great the father's love for the prodigal son was and how wholehearted his acceptance was when the boy finally found his way home. And it also helped me to realize that I had never been truly lost during those "prodigal" years. God had been with me all the time, providing what I would need to eventually find my way home to Him and to my true self. (When we find and understand our Father, we find and understand ourselves.)

You see, no matter how lost we may be, God always leaves breadcrumbs to lead us down the path to our destiny, our purpose, and our true identity in Him. For me, an important breadcrumb came when I saw my original birth certificate and came to the revelation that my biological mother had named me *Joseph Ambrose* after my father and his father before him. *Joseph* means "anointed one, sent of God," and *ambrose* means "one who paves the way." When I was born, my biological parent proclaimed through my name that I would be "an anointed one that will pave the way."

The discovery of this name not only drew me into a place of searching for who I truly was but also gave me a sudden strong desire to understand my lost roots. It led me into a deep study of Joseph, son of Jacob, from the Bible. I studied his journey from a child favored by his father to an outcast hated by his brothers, to a slave, to a prisoner, to a prime minister, and then to the man who saved all of the Middle East from the devastation of a seven-year drought. And I realized I identified with Joseph. While my sister and brother never hated me or sold me into slavery, I knew what it was like to have favor.

For one thing, when I was growing up, my parents always told me I was special. "You weren't just born. We *chose* you," they told me again and again. I also used to receive special attention from my Uncle Lou, who was my godfather. And while most of our family found themselves economically somewhere on the low end of middle class, Uncle Lou was a very successful restaurant owner in Los Angeles and lived very differently than my family. There was a time when I was sick at school and my Aunt Irene, Uncle Lou's wife, came to pick me up. Instead of parking at the gate, she pulled up directly in front of the school stairs in her brand-new baby blue T-bird and stepped out clad in a mink coat and high heels. Experiences such as that left lasting impressions on me.

I cannot tell you exactly why, but I had a special relationship with Uncle Lou. He shared his love of food with me even when I was very young. The other kids would eat hot dogs and burgers, but he always offered me a steak. Every time he greeted me, he would shake my hand and, in the process, pass off a five-, ten-, or twenty-dollar bill. He did not share this tradition with my siblings or my cousins, which inevitably created jealousy (just like Joseph). In fact, my aunt and uncle were consistently blessing me with little extras that outshone what they did for others. So, at a young age, I had to learn to manage this highly favored relationship dynamic.

In hindsight, being highly favored by my godfather was an excellent training ground to prepare me to walk in God's spiritual favor. All of us walk in a certain level of favor. It might seem unfair to some, but I have found that God's favor is often measured out or given according to the call on a person's life and how well he or she responds to it. As in the parable of the talents, when we prove ourselves able to multiply what God has given us, He gives us more, and with that comes a great expectation to produce even more for His kingdom.

> Who then is that faithful and wise steward, whom his master
> will make ruler over his household, to give them their por-
> tion of food in due season? Blessed is that servant whom his
> master will find so doing when he comes. . . . For everyone to
> whom much is given, from him much will be required; and
> to whom much has been committed, of him they will ask the
> more. (Luke 12:42–43, 48)

Stewardship of God's grace and purpose on our life is not just about managing your calling but also adapting your life socially so that you can live in your calling around others. It is most likely that you will experience the blessing and the favor of God especially in the areas of your gifting and purpose. Harnessing that is important to stepping into your destiny.

Joseph's young pride and his exuberance resulted in getting

thrown into a pit and sold into slavery, but ultimately his sense of calling resulted in good things despite the trouble it brought him. As he told his brothers later, "You meant evil against me; but God meant it for good, in order to bring it about as it is this day, to save many people alive" (Genesis 50:20). When the drought came, God used Joseph's strategic location and his favored position to save entire nations. Of course, he had to learn humility and wisdom first, which is what happened in the thirteen years between being sold a slave and becoming prime minister. Joseph learned how to make peace with the blessings that came with his heavenly calling.

It is not just enough to be blessed. We have to learn how to enjoy our blessings and to function productively at the same time. This is the true challenge. All of us are like Joseph in some way. We have dreams, aspirations, gifts, and talents, and all of us suffer envy, jealousy, and strife from other people as we try to discover and live into who we really are. It has been this way since Cain and Abel and is quite simply part of human nature and the human experience. But God is able to use every one of our life experiences to further His purposes if we let Him.

Every season has good and bad things that happen, but God allows both the positives and negatives in order to reveal treasures of purpose and destiny. Many of the things you have suffered through—I say "through" because we cannot escape suffering in the human experience, but we don't want to stop and set up camp in the middle of them either—may actually have been part of your treasure hunt. It is a good life exercise to look back at some of the more difficult seasons to recognize the life lessons learned in their midst. As we grow up in Christ, we should come to a place where we can thank God for both the good and the bad in the past because we know they both helped transform us into who we are today.

You may be walking through a very dark and troubled place right now. But I would encourage you, instead of trying to solve the problems of this season, to shift your focus and ask God what you should be learning in the midst of those problems. I have discovered that the act of seeking God for the lessons shortens the season of suffering. And more often than not, the sooner the lesson is learned, the more quickly the trial ends.

Scripture says that "the steps of a good [and righteous] man are ordered by the LORD" (Psalm 37:23). I have discovered this principle to be true—sometimes painfully so, because I haven't always understood what the Lord was doing at the time. I have labored for what I thought I wanted, only to discover it was not what I needed at all. I've invested a lot of energy and money into something that didn't pan out, only to find out later that the outcome I initially hoped for would have been a disaster. God does order our steps and protect us, but life is still a series of trials and tests and discoveries, and often we only see the ordering in hindsight. If you have a teachable spirit, however, all the trials and tests will become profitable for building your character—because true character is formed in our failures, not our successes.

When I look back, I can see that God was directing my steps—both the steps of favor and the steps of hurt and misunderstanding—to prepare me for my calling and my purpose today. He saw me in my full identity, while I saw only in part, "in a mirror, dimly" (1 Corinthians 13:12).

But at this new stage in my journey—newly reconnected with my biological father and my lost heritage—I had a new quest. It was time to find the half of me I hadn't known was missing until that day.

I would soon learn it was missing from the church as well.

ten

THE GOD WHO
KEEPS COVENANT

Every good gift and every perfect gift is from above,
and comes down from the Father of lights, with
whom there is no variation or shadow of turning.

—JAMES 1:17

NOT LONG AFTER I CONNECTED with my biological
father, while my mind continued to whirl with the revelation of
being Jewish, Christie and I found ourselves on a tour to Israel
with a few of our friends and a group of Taiwanese people. The
flight there was a long one, and by the time we landed in Tel Aviv,
I was wiped out. I felt like I was sleepwalking as we deplaned, got
our bags, and headed to the Dan Panorama Hotel on the beach. I
was so thankful that the tour wouldn't start until the next day, so
we had the night off.

As we got off the bus, I wasn't thinking about anything but laying my head onto a pillow. The tour leader, whom I'll call Jonathan, started giving instructions that I barely heard until he said, "Okay, everyone, go up to your rooms and we'll see you in the morning."

I started shuffling in that direction, but he waved me over. "Not you, Curt. I need to talk to you. The Lord is giving me a word for you."

Jonathan wasn't just a guy in charge of the trip, he was a leader well respected by our home church. Being pulled aside by him was a little like being called into the principal's office—or the district superintendent's office. So even though my body wanted to go one way, I nodded my head and went with him instead.

"Let's go down to the boardwalk." I dutifully turned and followed. We walked across the street from the hotel, down some stairs, and stepped out onto the wide promenade that lined the beach. The sea spread out before us. We were alone.

As we stood there, Jonathan put his hand on my shoulder, bowed his head, and started to pray under his breath. Then he raised his head, looked me in the eye, and began to tell the story of the rebirth of the nation of Israel, starting with the Holocaust.

He spared no details of what the Jews had suffered at the hands of the Nazis in the concentration camps—the experiments on children, the sexual abuse, the torture, all of it. He described how the German soldiers had sung Christmas carols and eaten cookies before warm fires as the Jews huddled together against the December cold, and ashes from the crematoriums fell like snow. He told me of the first people who had come to the land where we stood and fought for the right to stay, and what it had meant to them to once more have a nation that they could call their own.

It was an incredible journey of which I had only been marginally aware before. As Jonathan told it, I again felt tears sliding down my cheeks.

Then he told me of how alone the Jewish people felt in standing against all the nations around them and virtually the entire world as well. Few stood with them as true allies—even the United States, its most dedicated ally, often ran hot and cold with them, depending on the current political situation.

Finally, Jonathan shared about the burden he carried for the Jewish people and what God was moving him to do. The needs were so great. God's love for this group of people was so great. It broke my heart.

"Do you realize that the church was relatively asleep as Jewish families were being carted off to die in the gas chambers?" he went on. "And Satan plans to try to wipe out the Jews again before the end of the age, but the Lord is looking for those who will be a voice. He's looking for those who will rise up like John the Baptist—who will be a voice in the wilderness. Will you rise up and awaken the church?"

Then he took his hand from my shoulder and looked more deeply into my eyes, "I just felt like the Lord wanted me to share that with you. The Lord wants you to stay out here a bit and pray about this." Then he turned and walked back to the hotel.

I just stood there, overwhelmed. I'd never been to the Middle East, and as I stood there on the boardwalk, it struck me that I had no idea how safe this area was. Past reports of terrorist attacks flooded into my mind. Could I even remember the way back to our hotel? I realized I didn't know the language to be able to ask anyone. I was gripped by a momentary panic.

But Jonathan had instructed me to pray, so I pushed all that aside and started walking down toward the water. The beach in that area wasn't sandy, but it was full of large rocks used as a sea barrier—what they call riprap. I found a big chunk where I could sit with only the sea in front of me. It was so still; the only sounds I heard were the gentle lapping of the waves and an occasional seagull's cry. As I began to pray, images of what Jonathan had shared with me came back to my mind. And for the second time in my life, I felt like Jesus was standing right there with me.

Then, in the water, I spotted a school of fish—what looked like thousands of them, all silver and shimmering. They swam directly toward me, then made a U-turn and swam back in the direction from which they'd first appeared. It was a spectacular sight, and it went on for several minutes. I took it as a sign that this was a moment I was to remember, like the pillar of fire that had walked between the halves of the heifer, goat, and ram before Abraham.

I felt the presence of God come on me even more heavily. *"What do you want?"* He asked me.

I closed my eyes and put out my hands. "Make me a voice," I asked the Lord.

"You've heard my story from my prophet," He said to me.

"Yes, Lord. Make me a voice. Not on my watch—never again."

It was a phrase I had never heard before, but one I would hear repeatedly in the years to come. It was the pledge Israelis made in response to remembering the Holocaust. It would never happen again, not while they lived. They were willing to give their lives to make sure there will never be another holocaust.

Never again. That was the moment when my true identity and my calling first became clear to me, right there on that beach in Tel Aviv. God wanted me to make the same promise those Israelis had pledged their lives to. And in that moment I did.

God's heart for Israel was becoming my heart as well. I covenanted with God that I would be that voice for His chosen people, no matter what it might cost me, even if it cost me my life.

I will never forget that trip. But as I traveled to the ancient sites of Christianity and experienced the Jewish culture in the days that followed, I had a lot of questions. If God still loved the Jews as much as I had experienced sitting on that rock by the beach, why had the church so separated itself over the centuries from the Jewish people? Why the rift? What had happened? And what had we as Christians lost as a result?

To find the answers, I did the only thing I knew to do: I went to the Scriptures, and I began to study history.

In my first and subsequent trips to Israel—I have been there more than forty times now—I learned that the Jewish people are a people of covenant and that the roots of their heritage are deeply planted in covenant understanding. Once I realized that, I started studying about covenant and immediately saw that God isn't a covenant breaker.

> Therefore know that the LORD your God, He is God, the faithful God who keeps covenant and mercy for a thousand generations with those who love Him and keep His commandments. (Deuteronomy 7:9)

In fact, "He who keeps covenant" was literally part of the name of God Nehemiah and Daniel used to address Him:

> And I said: "I pray, LORD God of heaven, O great and awesome God, *You who keep Your covenant* and mercy with those who love You and observe Your commandments, please let Your ear be attentive and Your eyes open, that You may hear the prayer of Your servant." (Nehemiah 1:5–6)

> I prayed to the LORD my God, and made confession, and said, "O Lord, great and awesome God, who keeps His covenant and mercy with those who love Him, and with those who keep His commandments . . . hear the prayer of Your servant, and his supplications." (Daniel 9:4, 17)

I saw that the Bible is a history of covenants God established with human beings and that each specific covenant had its own place and significance in expressing who God is. Covenant, in other words, is the spiritual foundation of everything we do as believers. All else is built upon it, and it is what attaches us to heaven. Yet very few fully understand how it began or how it works—or does not work—in our lives today.

The Bible records eight biblical covenants between God and humanity—two conditional and six unconditional. Conditional covenants require certain conditions to be met for the covenant to remain valid. Unconditional covenants are basically "no strings attached" and continue in effect whether or not both parties live up to their agreements.

The first of the two conditional covenants is the Edenic covenant, also called the creation covenant, which was based on Adam and Eve not eating from the Tree of Knowledge of Good and Evil (Genesis 2–3). That covenant was broken, of course, and the garden of Eden is no more upon the earth.

The second is the Mosaic covenant, or Sinaitic covenant, so named because it was made with Moses on Mt. Sinai. This covenant is based on the law of Moses, which starts with the Ten Commandments and is woven throughout the first five books of the Bible—known by Christians as the Pentateuch and by Jews as the Torah.

The conditional nature of this covenant is clear. If God's people obeyed its laws, they would receive the blessings of Abraham[1] listed in Deuteronomy 28:

> Now it shall come to pass, *if you diligently obey the voice of the LORD your God, to observe carefully all His commandments which I command you today,* that the LORD your God will set you high above all nations of the earth. *And all these blessings shall come upon you and overtake you, because you obey the voice of the LORD your God.*

Blessed shall you be in the city, and blessed shall you be in the country.

Blessed shall be the fruit of your body, the produce of your ground and the increase of your herds, the increase of your cattle and the offspring of your flocks.

Blessed shall be your basket and your kneading bowl.

Blessed shall you be when you come in, and blessed shall you be when you go out.

The Lord will cause your enemies who rise against you to be defeated before your face; they shall come out against you one way and flee before you seven ways.

The Lord will command the blessing on you in your storehouses and in all to which you set your hand, and He will bless you in the land which the Lord your God is giving you.

The Lord will establish you as a holy people to Himself, just as He has sworn to you, *if you keep the commandments of the Lord your God and walk in His ways.*

Then all peoples of the earth shall see that you are called by the name of the Lord, and they shall be afraid of you.

And the Lord will grant you plenty of goods, in the fruit of your body, in the increase of your livestock, and in the produce of your ground, in the land of which the Lord swore to your fathers to give you.

The Lord will open to you His good treasure, the heavens, to give the rain to your land in its season, and to bless all the work of your hand.

You shall lend to many nations, but you shall not borrow.

And the Lord will make you the head and not the tail; you shall be above only, and not be beneath, *if you heed the commandments of the Lord your God, which I command you today, and are careful to observe them.*

So you shall not turn aside from any of the words which I

command you this day, to the right or the left, to go after other gods
to serve them (Deuteronomy 28:1–14).

If they didn't obey the laws, however, they not only would miss
out on the blessings; they would also receive the curses spelled out
in Deuteronomy 28:15–68. This covenant is still active today, with
some modifications made in the new covenant. (We'll look at this
in a few pages.)

The six unconditional covenants start with the Adamic covenant, made between God and Adam. It outlined the existence and
blessings of Adam and Eve, first in the garden and then out of the
garden after the fall.

The next is the Noahic covenant, made between God and
Noah. Its symbol is the rainbow, which signifies God's promise to
never again destroy the earth with flood.

The third covenant is the Abrahamic, the one we looked at in
chapter six; its tenets are summed up in Genesis 12:1–3. This covenant marks the time when God marked out a people for Himself.
God decided that He would call out a seed of Shem, one of Noah's
sons, and from him separate out a specific people and nation—the
children of Abraham—and form a special relationship with them.

The Abrahamic covenant was unilateral. God was the only
one who walked through the blood between the animals, so He
made sure the covenant was just about His promises to Abraham.
Abraham's faith was all that was necessary to seal his end of that
covenant; he didn't have to do anything but trust God. As a result,
Abraham's descendants will always be God's chosen people,
though He now calls them to the Messiah, Yeshua, for their fulfil-
ment, just as He calls the Gentiles.

The fourth unconditional covenant was again between God
and Moses as a representative of the Jewish people, but it was specifically tied to the scattering from and regathering of the Jewish

people in the promised land. It is called the land covenant. God made this covenant after Israel had wandered in the wilderness for forty years, after the rebellious generation that had refused to enter the promised land had passed away, and while the next generation was waiting on the plains of Moab to cross over into the promised land. Its tenets are set out in Deuteronomy 30:1–10.

> Now it shall come to pass, when all these things come upon you, the blessing and the curse which I have set before you, and you call them to mind among all the nations where the LORD your God drives you, and you return to the LORD your God and obey His voice, according to all that I command you today, you and your children, with all your heart and with all your soul, that the LORD your God will bring you back from captivity, and have compassion on you, and gather you again from all the nations where the LORD your God has scattered you. . . . Then the LORD your God will bring you to the land which your fathers possessed, and you shall possess it. He will prosper you and multiply you more than your fathers. (Deuteronomy 30:1–3, 5)

The fifth unconditional covenant is the one God made with King David. The Davidic covenant made four promises, but the main one was that a descendant of David would always be on the throne:

> When your days are fulfilled and you rest with your fathers, I will set up your seed after you, who will come from your body, and I will establish his kingdom. He shall build a house for My name, and I will establish the throne of his kingdom forever. I will be his Father, and he shall be My son. (2 Samuel 7:12–14)

This promise, of course, was fulfilled first in the lineage of kings of Israel, then Judah, who were David's offspring, and then ultimately in Jesus, who was of the house of David and the tribe of Judah.

Then there is the new covenant, which was instituted in the person of Jesus Christ as told in the Gospels and explored in detail throughout the rest of the New Testament. And there is a good deal of confusion as to the significance of that covenant in relationship to all the others. This confusion reveals itself today in two common beliefs Christians hold:

1. *The new covenant wiped out all previous covenants and is the only covenant God honors today.* This comes from a false doctrine called replacement theology, which we will look at later in more depth.
2. *The new covenant is for salvation only and has little to do with God's promises for life on the earth.* Yes, the promises of the Bible are ours, but God is sovereign, and how He honors His promises is completely up to Him.

These beliefs twist the truth so subtly that it's easy to see how they have misled many. In the next chapter we'll take a closer look at how they became so prevalent, but for now let's focus on how they have affected Christ's church.

On the surface, these false beliefs seem to be rooted in humility and to reject worldliness, but what they actually do is separate the church from her true heritage, inheritance, and place of authority as God's representatives on the earth. So in the end, they are just the opposite of what they claim to be. They have made the church self-righteous and an embracer of worldliness, and those in the pews today seem no holier than those in the streets. These beliefs have become our works and our religion, instead of His grace and His covenant promises. Something is terribly wrong, and I think it is a result of our disconnection with our true Judeo-Christian heritage. It's because we who accept Yeshua as Messiah have failed to recognize that the covenants God made with the Hebrew people are still in effect for us as well.

Once again, God is not a covenant breaker, and nothing Jesus did nullified any of the covenants made before He came. He fulfilled all their requirements so that the blessings of the Abrahamic and Mosaic covenants (the law) could be ours. As He Himself said,

> Do not think that I came to destroy the Law or the Prophets. I did not come to destroy but to fulfill. For assuredly, I say to you, till heaven and earth pass away, one jot or one tittle will by no means pass from the law till all is fulfilled. Whoever therefore breaks one of the least of these commandments, and teaches men so, shall be called least in the kingdom of heaven; but whoever does and teaches them, he shall be called great in the kingdom of heaven. (Matthew 5:17–19)

It's important to understand that the word *fulfill* in this context doesn't mean "end" or "complete." While it can mean that in certain contexts, here Jesus used it more to mean "carry out to the full," as we might say, "fulfilling the terms of a contract." Fulfilling the terms of a contract can mean that it ends, but that depends on the terms, right? What if it is an ongoing agreement—as most covenants are?

We don't typically wake up one day and tell our spouses, "Well, I've fulfilled my vows," and then walk away. In marriage, fulfilling our vows is a continual process that we will hopefully keep doing until the end of our days. And though covenants between individuals often end with the death of one of those in the agreement, even that isn't always true. David had a covenant pact of friendship with Jonathan, and 2 Samuel 9 shows that, after Jonathan's death, David carried that covenant forward by searching for a descendent of Jonathan to bless. And though marriage vows supposedly last only "till death do us part," the offspring of the couples who make those vows may go on for generations with that same last name, tied by an ancient marriage covenant.

In the same way, I believe, the covenants made between God and the Hebrew people continue forward to this day, fulfilled and transformed by Yeshua but still applicable for both the Jews and those of us in the church who are joint spiritual heirs. And as we fulfill our side of these covenants, we come into alignment with being blessed according to their tenets. Fulfilling my side is my responsibility, and it is the responsibility of the other party or parties to fulfill their side. I cannot demand that they fulfill their side because I have fulfilled mine, but I can remind them of their part by showing them I remember what was promised.

This, too, applies to the Jewish covenants that are part of our inheritance as Christians. The covenants still apply to us, but we need to be aware of them and even speak of them to God, reminding Him that we remember them. This is what God meant when He said through the prophet,

> Put Me in remembrance;
> Let us contend together;
> State your case, that you may be acquitted.
>
> (ISAIAH 43:26)

Why would we have to put God into remembrance of His Word, His promises, and His covenant? Because God does not want us changing His word and thus changing His instruction. He has not forgotten our heritage, and He wants to know that we haven't either.

"Come to Me in prayer," He is saying in this verse, "and don't just ask willy-nilly. Ask according to My promises. Show Me you know—and believe—what I've said to you. You do the small things; I'll do the big things. Show Me that you're in alignment under an open heaven and that you know the purpose behind the promises I've given you. Let's partner together in everything you do. Let's walk side by side toward the destiny I have set out for you." There is tremendous reward when we come before Him in this way, when we show that we remember our covenant and understand His promises.

Once we realize Jesus did not nullify the old covenants with the new covenant, but fulfilled them, and that they still apply to us today, the entire New Testament comes alive in completely new ways.

Yes, the new covenant replaces the requirements of the law in many ways—to the point that the book of Hebrews even calls it "obsolete" (8:13)—but that is only for those who actually step into the new covenant. Jews become complete by coming to the Messiah, Jesus, who is the promise and fulfillment of Old Testament law and prophecies. But God has not abandoned the Jews who haven't yet discovered those truths. He is still reaching out to them every day.

For those of us who have embraced the new covenant, strict obedience to the law is replaced with grace and forgiveness, as Galatians 3:13–14 explains: "Christ has redeemed us from the curse of the law, having become a curse for us (for it is written, 'Cursed is everyone who hangs on a tree'), that the blessing of Abraham might come upon the Gentiles in Christ Jesus."

Through the cross, Christ redeemed us from the requirements of the law. But—this is so important to recognize—He did not remove us from the *effects* of the law.

The cross is most definitely about salvation and going to

heaven, but because we are still under the older covenants, we have access to other blessings as well. All the blessings of the Abrahamic and Mosaic covenants as recorded in Deuteronomy 28 are ours, blessings that will help us prosper and make us more effective in our callings *here on earth.*

According to the Talmud, the authoritative body of religious tradition, there are 613 laws or *mitzvot* (dos or don'ts) recorded in the Old Testament. The gift of the blood of Jesus fulfills the requirements of all 613 laws and therefore releases us to receive all 613 associated blessings in our lives. That is what makes us "the head and not the tail" (Deuteronomy 28:13).

But remember, Deuteronomy 28 is all about cause and effect: "I will bless you *if . . .*" or "I will curse you *if . . .*" That *if* factor still applies to us, too, and represents a choice: "I call heaven and earth as witnesses today against you, that I have set before you life and death, blessing and cursing; therefore choose life, that both you and your descendants may live" (Deuteronomy 30:19).

How we choose is our covenantal response to God. It is the tangible demonstration of our faith. We do because we believe, but our blessing depends on our choice to do:

> Show me your faith without your works, and I will show you
> my faith by my works. . . . Was not Abraham our father jus-
> tified by works *[obedience]* when he offered Isaac his son on
> the altar? Do you see that faith was working together with
> his works, and by works faith was made perfect? And the
> Scripture was fulfilled which says, "Abraham believed God,
> and it was accounted to him for righteousness." And he was
> called the friend of God. You see then that a man is justified
> by works, and not by faith only. . . . For as the body without
> the spirit is dead, so faith without works is dead also. (James
> 2:18, 21–24, 26)

Notice this passage speaks of Abraham as "the friend of God"—covenant language again. Abraham was "justified" (came into alignment with the covenant, came under an open heaven) through faith that was demonstrated and "made perfect" (fulfilled) "by works"—that is, through obedience.

Faith and grace, in other words, do not replace covenant. Faith and grace activate covenant. And God is still working today through the covenants He made with His people thousands of years ago. Nothing has been nullified.

Yes, when we come into the New Testament, we come into "a better covenant" (Hebrews 7:22 NIV), but it's hard to understand exactly why it is better without understanding the heritage and promises it encompasses, fulfills, and gives access to.

Think of it this way. Gravity is a law. The laws of aerodynamics that make airplanes fly overcome gravity. But gravity doesn't change. It's still in effect.

God even told the Jews to look for the day that the new covenant would fulfill and improve on (but not nullify) the Mosaic covenant:

> Behold, the days are coming, says the LORD, when I will make a new covenant with the house of Israel and with the house of Judah—not according to the covenant that I made with their fathers in the day that I took them by the hand to lead them out of the land of Egypt, My covenant which they broke, though I was a husband to them, says the LORD. But this is the covenant that I will make with the house of Israel after those days, says the LORD: I will put My law in their minds, and write it on their hearts; and I will be their God, and they shall be My people. No more shall every man teach his neighbor, and every man his brother, saying, "Know the LORD," for they all shall know Me, from the least of them to the greatest of them, says the LORD.

For I will forgive their iniquity, and their sin I will remember
no more. (Jeremiah 31:31–34)

God has not broken any of His other covenants either—they
are still in play. That is why, after almost two thousand years,
the Jews came back to Israel. No other people group has ever
experienced anything close to that. God was honoring His land
covenant with them as well as His promises to Abraham. He was
also setting the pieces on the board for Daniel's "seventieth week"
and the events of the book of Revelation, which are almost all
focused on the salvation of the Jewish people.

God has not abandoned His people, the Jews, and neither
should the church, though in many ways we have. It's time for us
to return and reclaim the heritage we share and bless those who
hold dear the prophecies of our King as we should.

In the last twenty-five years of ministry, the biggest challenge
I have faced in sharing this message about our covenant heritage is
getting Christians to understand how *grace through Jesus Christ* and
obedience to the law are one. The word *law*—or *torah* in Hebrew—
translates out as "instruction." And God has never changed His
instruction, because He doesn't change:

For I *am* the LORD, *I do not change.* (Malachi 3:6)

Because God wanted to make the *unchanging nature of his purpose* very clear to the heirs of what was promised, he confirmed
it with an oath. (Hebrews 6:17 NIV)

Understanding the power of the blood of Jesus to expunge
sin as if it were never committed is supreme grace—the ultimate
grace that all of us need. When sin is annulled and removed,

health and prosperity always have a place to prosper in the human soul, and that is the truest hope of the gospel of Jesus Christ.

The church, however, does not understand the way grace works in the Old Testament covenants. Basically, it depends on our approach to the instruction. Following it with faith and love releases grace. Following it with legalism and obligation annuls grace. Grace prospers where people follow God's instruction because they are motivated by love and honor, not religious obligation.

True grace is based on a relationship with God as our heavenly Father and not as a taskmaster constantly chastising us about what's right and what's wrong. God's judgment is a friend of those who desire right standing with Him because the judgment removes the roots of death that bring destruction. Judgment from a legalistic standpoint, however, binds us to those dead roots.

God's character and nature are unchanging. He is a God of love. He *is* love. And His historic testimony of victory—covered in compassion, mercy, and grace—deserves our trust and the time and focus it takes to dig into our complete heritage so we can know Him more completely for the fullness of who He is.

You have open doors, windows, and opportunities in your life that have not yet been identified. There are things about you and your faith that are buried in history and that you may know nothing about, and discovering these things can be one of the most exciting quests you can ever embark upon. Your hunger for truth—the truth about who you are and who and what you are rooted in—is just the beginning of laying a foundation for identity, success, and legacy. The void you may feel and the ache you may have for more will propel you into purpose.

I know that has been true for me. The revelation that God desired to establish His covenant and His promises in and through my life and lifestyle profoundly changed my thinking about how a human being interacts with a sovereign God. Quite simply: when God so generously sent His only Son to improve and empower God's covenant mandates by expunging sin at the cross and tearing the veil that separated us from His *shekinah* glory, thereby giving access to His presence to all who would call on the name of the Lord, He paved the path for the return of all the peoples of the earth to Himself. He made it possible for anyone who comes to Him to lead a life of identity, destiny, and power.

The power of covenant that changes identity and purpose— and thereby creates thoughts, actions, and deeds in line with covenant—has to be revealed in and through a mental cleansing of attitudes and perception to allow us to see that our unchanging God is, in fact, the supreme Giver. He is not a taker. Every good and perfect gift comes from Him.

It's time we stepped into the lives Christ paid the ultimate sacrifice to give us. It is, literally, what we were made for.

eleven

THE CHURCH
OF THE NEW
TESTAMENT

> *For if the firstfruit is holy, the lump is also holy; and*
> *if the root is holy, so are the branches. And if some of*
> *the branches were broken off, and you, being a wild*
> *olive tree, were grafted in among them, and with*
> *them became a partaker of the root and fatness of the*
> *olive tree, do not boast against the branches. But if*
> *you do boast, remember that you do not support the*
> *root, but the root supports you.*
>
> —ROMANS 11:16–18

THERE WAS A BANNER THAT HUNG on our church wall
at Grace Church in Washington. It read: "Seek first the kingdom

of God and His righteousness, and all these things shall be added to you" (Matthew 6:33).

Every time I think about that banner, I'm reminded of a message our pastor at Grace shared with us. The focus of his message was that God's kingdom needs to be the priority of our hearts, that it was not a mental issue but a heart issue.

Pastor Steve's message challenged me, and the words of Jesus so boldly proclaimed on that church banner began to sink deep into my heart. It remains a life scripture for me today. But my understanding of that verse has grown tremendously since that day because of my studies in Christianity's Hebrew heritage.

When Jesus came, everything He said was in context of Jewish culture, Jewish traditions, and the Jewish belief system. Yes, He took things up a significant notch—you only have to read the Sermon on the Mount to see that—but the foundation was still Jewish. So when we interpret His words through a Western philosophical lens, we change the meaning of much of what He said. We end up with a diluted or warped understanding of His words. While the meanings haven't been so lost that His words and actions fail to save, the change is significant enough that we often fail to be who He has called us to be on the earth. Losing the fullness and context of Jesus' words, we've lost much of the authority they were meant to confer on us.

Take, for example, the word *righteousness* in Matthew 6:33. When I first heard Pastor Steve preach about this verse, my take on this word was more Greek than Jewish. I thought it meant keeping all the rules. I was *righteous*—"right with God"—to the degree that I was "a law-abiding citizen" of heaven, and any rewards I received for that would be based on my performance. Even though Pastor Steve was preaching grace—our church was called Grace Church, after all—I couldn't get a performance-based idea of rightness with God out of my paradigm. I saw everything through the lens of meritocracy and thought of blessings from heaven as almost like a points-and-rewards system.

This was not conscious on my part. I talked a lot about grace and unmerited favor and quoted Scripture verbatim, but my understanding of all those words was built on Western philosophy—Greek and Roman thinking, with an overlay of the Protestant work ethic. I assumed that if I did good things, God would reward me with blessings; if I didn't, He would withhold them. My thinking was legalistic, not covenantal.

As I grew in my understanding of my own Jewish roots, however, I learned that the Hebrew word for righteousness—*tzedakah*—means something very different. It could be translated as "justice" and is closely associated with acts of charity and giving; its root word is *tzedek*, which also means "fairness."

So when we read Matthew 6:33 in the context of how Jesus' audience would have understood His words, we understand that He was telling them to seek first the kingdom of God and His *justice*—His fairness—hence the Jewish tradition of giving *tzedakah*, which is the giving of financial alms or aid and assistance to the poor, the needy, or those who have been denied justice. It's literally doing things that facilitate empowerment, equality, and freedom for all. Seeking His righteousness is an active action of promoting social justice on the earth, not just keeping rules and performing as Christians.

Just look at how Lois Tverberg, author of *Reading the Bible with Rabbi Jesus*, described the word:

> It may surprise us, then, that the phrase, *tzedkot Adonai* (righteous acts of God) in Jewish versions of the Bible is translated as "kindnesses," "abundant benevolences," "gracious acts," and "gracious deliverances." This is because the word *tzedakah* means more than just legal correctness—it refers to covenantal

faithfulness, often resulting in rescuing those in distress and showing mercy to sinners.

This is why King David says to God, "Judge me, O LORD my God, according to Your righteousness, and do not let them rejoice over me" (Psalm 35:24). He is actually appealing to God's mercy to those under his covenant, rather than his legal judgments.[1]

From this Jewish perspective, then, one would better read Matthew 6:33 in this way: "Seek first the kingdom and the righteous acts of God—seek first kindness, seek first abundant benevolences, seek first gracious acts and deliverances—and all these other things will then be added to you."

Read in this way, Matthew 6:33 requires a daily walk of faith that still challenges me to this day. But it's not about believing the right things or even being right; it's about *doing* right—justice—and right is never completely done. This echoes Micah 6:8:

> He has shown you, O man, what is good;
> And what does the LORD require of you
> But to do justly,
> To love mercy,
> And to walk humbly with your God?

Seeking first His righteousness is thus a lifestyle commitment, one I never regretted making. It is certainly not for the faint of heart or for those who desire a boring existence, because it demands a life of faithful risk and daring, not merely sitting back and being right. But it bears the fruit of supernatural results according to the Word: "and all these things shall be added to you."

Now, if this is true of this one verse—and this one word that is so crucial to our understanding of being in covenant with

God—we should probably ask what else we're misunderstanding in the words of the New Testament, especially those of Jesus.

If we want to interpret Scripture correctly, context is incredibly important. Who was being spoken or written to matters because shared understandings are commonly not included in the writing. If you lived where we now do in Oklahoma and I mentioned "OSU," you would probably assume correctly that I was referring to the Oklahoma State University Cowboys and was probably talking about football. That's just the way Oklahoma is. The same could not be said, however, if I were in Ohio or Oregon. I would have to spell out what I meant more clearly if I said "OSU" in those states; otherwise, I'd be speaking in the wrong context and cause some cultural confusion.

In the same way, there are certain aspects of living wisely that Jesus didn't have to mention in His stories because His audience shared His culture and understood what He meant. For instance, many of His parables (the sower, wheat and tares, the mustard seed, and more) used farming as their basis, and since His audience was familiar with the farming techniques of that day, He didn't have to explain them as we sometimes have to when teaching about those same parables today.

When Jesus told about the rich fool who was going to build bigger storehouses to horde his wealth (Luke 12:16–21), the story hit home because every farmer listening to him had multiple storehouses at home. Farmers did that so that they could store up grain and let their land rest every seventh and fiftieth year in obedience to Scripture (Leviticus 25:1–7). Today, however, when most people don't even have enough in their savings accounts to cover a month of expenses, we tend to read that parable very differently.

It's like our "zero" is in a different place. Ours is at literal zero, while theirs was at a place where they could live for two years without needing to plant or harvest anything. Today, many Christians act as if having anything at all laid away for the future reflects greed or a lack of faith, while to the Jews of Jesus' day, it would reflect wisdom. But we might miss that if we are interpreting things through our culture and age and not through the cultural context in which Jesus told His stories.

Our skewed cultural lens can also cause us to misunderstand God's purpose in sending Jesus to the Jewish people. He wasn't making one last desperate attempt to save them, with the understanding that God would be done with them if they didn't accept Him. No, Jesus came to the Jews because He intended to build the church upon the foundation of Judaism. Jesus came and taught the Jews to seed the church, and then He released the church into Judaism to be born.

The first church was completely Jewish after all, and it remained that way until the times recorded in Acts 8, when Philip began converting Samaritans, whom the Jews considered half-breeds. And the church didn't start including Gentiles until the times recorded in Acts 10, which scholars believe was about seven to ten years after Christ's ascension, when He had given orders to His followers to be "witnesses to Me in Jerusalem, and in all Judea and Samaria, and to the end of the earth" (Acts 1:8).

Notice the progression Jesus gave for preaching the gospel: to the Jews first (in Jerusalem and all Judea), then to the half-Jews (the Samaritans), then to the rest of the world (the Gentiles). The book of Acts records that they did just that—beginning in Jerusalem (Acts 2–7), reaching out to Judea and Samaria and to the Ethiopian eunuch (Acts 8), then to Gentile proselytes (Acts 10), and finally to Antioch and beyond (the calling of Saul in Acts 9, and then the missionary journeys recorded in Acts 11 and beyond).

The apostle Paul also recorded this progression when he wrote: "I am not ashamed of the gospel, for it is the power of God to salvation for everyone who believes, *to the Jew first* and also to the Greek" (Romans 1:16).

Never in any of this did Jesus tell the apostles that they were to reject the Jews because the Jews had rejected Him. He never said anything remotely like that. Instead, He always used Judaism as the starting point from which to reach out to the other nations and ethnicities of the world. To use the apostle Paul's analogy, He wasn't replacing the Jews with the Gentiles, but grafting the Gentiles into the cultivated "olive tree" of Israel:

> I say then, has God cast away His people? Certainly not! . . . I say then, have [the Jews] stumbled that they should fall? Certainly not! But through their fall, *to provoke them to jealousy*, salvation has come to the Gentiles. Now if their fall is riches for the world, and their failure riches for the Gentiles, *how much more their fullness!* . . .
>
> *For if the firstfruit is holy, the lump is also holy; and if the root is holy, so are the branches.* And if some of the branches were broken off, and you, being a wild olive tree, were grafted in among them, and with them became a partaker of the root and fatness of the olive tree, do not boast against the branches. But if you do boast, remember that you do not support the root, but the root supports you.
>
> For I do not desire, brethren, that you should be ignorant of this mystery, lest you should be wise in your own opinion. (Romans 11:1, 11–12, 16–18, 25)

Paul was writing to Gentile Christians here, and he warned them explicitly of the danger of straying from Jewish thinking and culture and thereby moving out into their own opinions. The Gentiles had been grafted into the new covenant, but the Jews had not been "grafted out." Judaism was still the root—"the lump"—of God's relationship with humanity. It was where He started, and it is still the fundamental heritage of all who are in covenant with God.

Paul then went on to issue a further warning:

> You will say then, "Branches were broken off that I might be grafted in." Well said. Because of unbelief they were broken off, and you stand by faith. Do not be haughty, but fear. For if God did not spare the natural branches, He may not spare you either. Therefore consider the goodness and severity of God: on those who fell, severity; but toward you, goodness, if you continue in His goodness. Otherwise you also will be cut off. And they also, if they do not continue in unbelief, will be grafted in, *for God is able to graft them in again.* For if you were cut out of the olive tree which is wild by nature, and were grafted contrary to nature into a cultivated olive tree, *how much more will these, who are natural branches, be grafted into their own olive tree?* (Romans 11:19–24)

But what of Acts 15? What of Romans 14? What of grace instead of Jewish law? Many read these passages as a desertion of Judaism and the Old Testament. But that was never the intention of the apostles, who were Jews grounded in Jewish thought and who remembered Jesus' statement that He hadn't come to destroy the law and the prophets, but to fulfill them (Matthew 5:17–19).

The question in these passages was not whether Christianity would be a Jewish or Gentile religion but how much of the Jewish law would be required to be considered Christian. (And remember, it wasn't even until Acts 11:26 that anyone was called a Christian.) One faction of the early church, called the Judaizers, insisted that new believers had to follow all the tenets of the Jewish law, including circumcision, the sign of the Abrahamic covenant.

Others, including Peter, Paul, and Barnabas, insisted that there were more significant indicators that we belonged to God. The dispute grew so heated that a meeting of the apostles and elders was called in Jerusalem. And at that meeting Peter weighed in with the question of which was more a sign of God's acceptance of the Gentiles: circumcision or being filled with the Holy Spirit?

> Now the apostles and elders came together to consider this matter. And when there had been much dispute, Peter rose up and said to them: "Men and brethren, you know that a good while ago God chose among us, that by my mouth the Gentiles should hear the word of the gospel and believe. So God, who knows the heart, acknowledged them by giving them the Holy Spirit, just as He did to us, and made no distinction between us and them, purifying their hearts by faith. Now therefore, why do you test God by putting a yoke on the neck of the disciples which neither our fathers nor we were able to bear? But we believe that through the grace of the Lord Jesus Christ we shall be saved in the same manner as they." (Acts 15:6–11)

Paul and Barnabas then testified that they had not seen God hold anything back from the Gentile believers either. And finally, after listening to all, James declared:

> And with this the words of the prophets agree, just as it is
>   written:
> "After this I will return
> And will rebuild the tabernacle of David,
> which has fallen down;
> I will rebuild its ruins,
> And I will set it up;
> So that the rest of mankind may seek the LORD,

> Even all the Gentiles who are called by
> My name,
> Says the LORD who does all these things."

Known to God from eternity are all His works. Therefore I judge that we should not trouble those from among the Gentiles who are turning to God, but that we write to them to abstain from things polluted by idols, from sexual immorality, from things strangled, and from blood. For Moses has had throughout many generations those who preach him in every city, being read in the synagogues every Sabbath. (Acts 15:15–21)

In this they declared that through Yeshua the new covenant fulfilled the requirements of the Abrahamic and other covenants but had not nullified them (Ephesians 2:12; Matthew 5:17). The sign of the new covenant was to be "circumcision of the heart" by accepting Jesus as the Messiah, not the circumcision of Abraham. Christians would be known by their acts of faith and love, not by any other outward signs. Paul wrote of this in his letter to the Romans:

> For he is not a Jew who is one outwardly, nor is circumcision that which is outward in the flesh; but he is a Jew who is one inwardly; and circumcision is that of the heart, in the Spirit, not in the letter; whose praise is not from men but from God.
>
> What advantage then has the Jew, or what is the profit of circumcision? Much in every way! Chiefly because to them were committed the oracles of God. For what if some did not believe? Will their unbelief make the faithfulness of God without effect? Certainly not! Indeed, let God be true but every man a liar. (Romans 2:28–3:4)

Note that Paul emphasized that the new covenant "circumcision of the heart" does not mean God had rejected the Jews or nullified His covenant with them. To Him they were still the people of the prophets—the same prophets who had foretold Jesus' coming. Paul made the forceful point that even if the Jews were unfaithful to their covenants with God, He would not be unfaithful to them in return.

We see this emphasis on heart attitudes over outward displays repeated in Romans 14, where Paul discussed such loaded issues as diet and the celebration of holidays:

> One person esteems one day above another; another esteems
> every day alike. Let each be fully convinced in his own mind.
> He who observes the day, observes it to the Lord; and he who
> does not observe the day, to the Lord he does not observe it. . . .
> For none of us lives to himself, and no one dies to himself. For
> if we live, we live to the Lord; and if we die, we die to the Lord.
> Therefore, whether we live or die, we are the Lord's. . . .
> So then each of us shall give account of himself to God.
> Therefore let us not judge one another anymore, but rather
> resolve this, not to put a stumbling block or a cause to fall in
> our brother's way. (Romans 14:5–8, 12–13)

Paul declared that "keeping a day" to the Lord was good, just as *not* "keeping a day," if both were "to the Lord." All God's people were to follow their consciences concerning these things. And yet the early church—for several centuries, in fact—followed its conscience to celebrate the Jewish holidays and remember the Jewish Sabbath, as had Jesus throughout His ministry.

If the holidays—the "holy days"—of the Jewish calendar were suddenly unimportant, why had God bothered to honor them with events like the coming of the Holy Spirit on Pentecost, the

Jewish holiday called *Shavuot*, fifty days after Passover? These observances were so ingrained in the practices of the apostles that Luke didn't record them in the book of Acts. Here again we see a Jewish cultural foundation that is so central to the early church that it was barely mentioned in most of the New Testament.

Take, as another example, the early church's practice of "meeting from house to house" as their numbers exploded.

> So continuing daily with one accord in the temple, and break-
> ing bread from house to house, they ate their food with
> gladness and simplicity of heart, praising God and having favor
> with all the people. . . . And daily in the temple, and in every
> house, they did not cease teaching and preaching Jesus as the
> Christ. (Acts 2:46–47; 5:42)

Notice that, first of all, the Jews did not forsake the temple as a gathering place. They went there daily. And second, when they broke bread "from house to house" and "in every house," what night of the week do you think that happened?

Historians tell us that it was usually on Friday evenings, not just randomly throughout the week. Why? Because it was already their practice to gather on Friday evenings to welcome the coming of the Jewish Sabbath at sundown. Even today, Jews observe *Shabbat* from sundown on Friday to sundown on Saturday. Practically speaking, they would have already had that on their calendars as a night to gather. Besides, the usual workweek in that culture was Sunday through Friday, so when else would they have met? They certainly didn't have church on Sunday mornings when everyone around them was going to work!

It wasn't until more than a century later that the church would start considering Sunday—the day of the week when Christ rose from the dead—as their Sabbath or "day of rest." It wouldn't become common practice until the fourth century. Until then, the house gatherings were almost certainly *Shabbat* gatherings. But the culture of the early church was so completely Jewish that, again, the New Testament writers didn't point it out.

What we do see in the New Testament accounts is the grafting of the Gentiles into a Jewish church, not the grafting out of the Jews. God meant for there to be no more distinction: "There is neither Jew nor Greek, there is neither slave nor free, there is no male and female, for you are all one in Christ Jesus. And if you are Christ's, then you are Abraham's offspring, heirs according to promise" (Galatians 3:28–29 ESV).

But instead, as we shall see in the next chapter, in the centuries following Jesus, Rome had many problems with the church and wanted to capture and conquer it in the same way it had all other lands and cultures. Jews were a constant thorn in their side, even after the destruction of the temple in AD 70 and the exile of the Jews from Jerusalem by the emperor Hadrian in AD 135. In the years to come, Rome would continue to persecute the church and try to overcome the tenacity of those who joined it. It eventually did this by accepting Christianity but cutting it away from its Jewish roots. And since then, despite its achievements, the church has also been suffering an identity crisis.

When we Christians neglect our Jewish heritage, we become like a person who has a fruit tree but cares only for the branches and never pays attention to the trunk or roots. Anyone who knows anything about trees knows that it's the watering and feeding of the roots that causes trees to produce their best fruit.

Can you imagine what would happen if you watered the branches of your tree but did everything you could to keep them away from the influence of their roots? That's no way to get fruit, let alone keep the tree alive.

twelve

OUR STOLEN
HERITAGE

> For I do not desire, brethren, that you should be
> ignorant of this mystery, lest you should be wise
> in your own opinion, that blindness in part has
> happened to Israel until the fullness of the Gentiles has
> come in. And so all Israel will be saved, as it is written:
>
> "The Deliverer will come out of Zion,
> And He will turn away ungodliness from Jacob;
> For this is My covenant with them,
> When I take away their sins."
>
> —ROMANS 11:25–27

THE FIRST-CENTURY CHURCH, as we have seen, was essentially Jewish with Gentiles grafted in. But a strange thing began to occur after the temple in Jerusalem was destroyed and Jewish leaders were exiled from their homeland. Very slowly and without plan, the center of the church shifted from Jerusalem to Rome. Both Peter and Paul had died in Rome sometime around AD 66, meaning two of the church's most important pillars were buried in Rome, and the church there thrived despite continual persecution.

Still, at least through the writing of the last book of the Bible and the death of the last apostle (John, around AD 100), Christianity remained intertwined with its Jewish roots and, in many places, still not seen as a distinctly different religion. With Christianity not yet having a clearly organized, "orthodox" Christian leadership to say who was in or out, and with the Jewish leadership disbanded, the two pressed on intermingled for the first three centuries after Christ's resurrection and ascension.

At some point during that time, however—it's hard to tell exactly why or when, since many of the early church writings of this time have been lost, especially those that kept Christianity "grafted" into its Hebrew roots—what we now call replacement theology began to creep into Christian thought. This was the idea that the true people of God—the true Israel—was no longer one of flesh, but one of faith. Replacement theology teaches that the Christian church has fully replaced Israel in God's mind and the Jewish people as God's chosen. It also teaches that all promises and prophecies have thereby been transferred from Israel to the church and that therefore the state of Israel and the Jewish people no longer have an active role in Bible prophecy but are simply a political accident.

Some scholars also call this the "doctrine of rejection" of the Jews, and we see it as early as in a letter from Bishop Ignatius of Antioch (ca. 35–108) to the Magnesians (in modern-day Turkey),

"To profess Jesus Christ while continuing to follow Jewish customs is an absurdity. The Christian faith does not look to Judaism, Judaism looks to Christianity, in which every other race and tongue that confesses a belief in God has not been comprehended."[1]

In his *Dialogue with Trypho* (a Jew), Justin Martyr (ca. 100–165) asserted that the Scriptures were "not yours, but ours."[2] The early church father Irenaeus (ca. 130–202) wrote, in his *Against Heresies*:

> [The Jews] indeed, had they been cognizant of [Christians'] future existence, and that we should use these proofs from the Scriptures, would themselves never have hesitated to burn their own Scriptures, which do declare that all other nations partake of [eternal] life, and *show that they who boast themselves as being the house of Jacob and the people of Israel, are disinherited from the grace of God.*[3] (emphasis added)

Tertullian (ca. 160–220) is credited with writing, "God has rejected the Jews in favor of the Christians,"[4] and Eusebius of Caesarea (ca. 263–339) with, "The promises of the Hebrew Scriptures are now for the Christians and not the Jews—but the curses are for the Jews."[5] Origen of Alexandria (ca. 184–253) wrote:

> We say with confidence that [the Jews] will never be restored to their former condition. For they committed a crime of the most unhallowed kind, in conspiring against the Saviour of the human race. . . . It accordingly behooved that city where Jesus underwent these sufferings to perish utterly, and the Jewish nation to be overthrown, and the invitation to happiness offered them by God to pass to others — the Christians, I mean.[6]

Despite all this, some in the church still looked favorably upon the Jews and Judaism. Augustine of Hippo (354–430) wrote in his *City of God* that the Jews were not the enemies of Christianity but unknowing witnesses to the truth of Old Testament prophecies about Christ, and as such should be respected and protected:

> By the evidence of their own scriptures they bear witness for us that we have not fabricated the prophecies about Christ. . . . It follows that when the Jews do not believe in our scriptures, their scriptures are fulfilled in them, while they read them with blind eyes. . . . It is in order to give this testimony which, in spite of themselves, they supply for our benefit by their possession and preservation of those books [of the Old Testament] that they are themselves dispersed among all nations, wherever the Christian church spreads. . . . Hence the prophecy in the Book of Psalms: "Slay them not, lest they forget your law; scatter them by your might."[7]

But the die against the Jews was ultimately cast when the Roman emperor Constantine the Great (306–337) embraced Christianity and made it the state religion of Rome. Over the years that followed, the catholic (universal) church became Roman, though not Roman Catholic, exactly. (The catholic church was more a victim of Rome than a perpetrator, though it would perpetuate that Roman influence in the centuries to come.) In essence, the wild olive branches of the church were broken off of the trunk of Judaism and grafted into the logic and philosophy of Greece and the pagan mythology of Rome. And the church was cut off from her true roots and heritage and grafted into the foundations of Western culture.

It was during this time that the early church councils began to make rulings deliberately separating Christian and Jewish observances. The First Council of Nicaea, convened by Emperor

Constantine in AD 325, definitely cut the cord with one of the most important cultural aspects of Judaism: the calendar that set the dates for holy days. The Council of Antioch that convened in 341 prohibited Christians from celebrating Passover with the Jews, and the Council of Laodicea (c. 363) barred Christians from observing the Jewish Sabbath. (It was not uncommon for Christians at that time to observe both Sunday worship and the Sabbath service on Friday evenings.) It also forbade Christians from receiving gifts from Jews or *matzo* (flat, unleavened bread) during Jewish festivals.

The reason that Christians and Jews worship on separate days was originally rooted in the transition from the Jewish lunar calendar in the Constantine period, when church authorities under Constantine outlawed the observance of Passover by Christians and began combining the resurrection testimony of Jesus with the celebration of the spring solstice, which, for Rome, had long honored the fertility goddess Ishtar. Historian Heinrich Graetz explained the transition from Jewish Passover—the week of Christ's crucifixion and resurrection—to Easter:

> At the Council of Nice [Nicaea] the last thread was snapped which connected Christianity to its parent stock. The festival of Easter had up till now been celebrated for the most part at the same time as the Jewish Passover, and indeed upon the days calculated and fixed by the Synhedrion [Sanhedrin] in Judea for its celebration; *but in future its observance was to be rendered altogether independent of the Jewish calendar.* "For it is unbecoming beyond measure that on this holiest of festivals we should follow the customs of the Jews. Henceforward let us have nothing in common with this odious people; our Saviour has shown us another path. It would indeed be absurd if the Jews were able to boast that we are not in a position to celebrate the Passover

without the aid of their rules (calculations)." These remarks are attributed to the Emperor Constantine . . . [and became] the guiding principle of the Church *which was now to decide the fate of the Jews.*[8] (emphasis added)

Until the Council of Nicaea, in other words, Passover was still being celebrated by both Jewish and Gentile Christians. The choice to separate was a political, human choice, not a God choice. The letter that resulted from the Council of Nicaea concluded by saying:

> We also send you the good news of the settlement concerning the holy pasch [Passover], namely that in answer to your prayers this question also has been resolved. All the brethren in the East who have hitherto followed the Jewish practice will henceforth observe the custom of the Romans and of yourselves and of all of us who from ancient times have kept Easter together with you. Rejoicing then in these successes and in the common peace and harmony and in the cutting off of all heresy, welcome our fellow minister, your bishop Alexander, with all the greater honour and love. He has made us happy by his presence, and despite his advanced age has undertaken such great labour in order that you too may enjoy peace.[9]

While this issue is not one that denies salvation to believers, it is an area where the Christian church has been robbed of the heritage blessing of putting our feet under the Father's table.

In addition to that, the transition from the Jewish lunar calendar (the calendar used throughout the Bible) to the Julian calendar (the Roman calendar introduced under Julius Caesar around AD 46) changed the very structure of the basic week. You can see this even today in Israel, where the workweek begins on Sunday and ends at sundown on Friday. This structure was birthed with creation, as recorded in Genesis 1 and 2. It is quite clear from this text that the seventh day was set apart and sanctified as the holy day of rest. (When something is set apart, it is distinguished or noted as different from the others in comparison.)

> Thus the heavens and the earth, and all the host of them, were finished. And on the seventh day God ended His work which He had done, and He rested on the seventh day from all His work which He had done. Then God blessed the seventh day and sanctified it, because in it He rested from all His work which God had created and made. (Genesis 2:1–3)

In the same year as the Council of Nicaea, Constantine instituted a ruling that his urban subjects should observe their day of rest on Sunday, which many Christians had come to see as "the Lord's day." As mentioned above, however, they commonly observed the Jewish Sabbath as well, until that was outlawed by the Council of Laodicea.

The official establishment of Sunday as the official day of rest was followed by the institution of Christmas as the celebration of the birth of Christ or the birth of the Son on December 25. Coincidently (or not so coincidently), that date marked the winter solstice, when the sun was at its lowest point in the sky and about to begin its annual comeback. This was the day the followers of the sun god worshipped as the birth of the sun.

With these changes by Constantine and his successors, in league with bishops gathered in councils, the westernization of the church and the resulting disconnect from Jewish heritage was fully established. It would continue on that path through subsequent centuries, and the resulting damage would be incalculable. The spirit that came upon the men at the councils during this period, the spirit that caused them to make decisions that separated generations from the blessings of God, was not the Holy Spirit. It was a spirit that was anti-anointing, anti-blessing, anti-Christ, anti-Semitic, and anti-spiritual root. And the consequence of that spirit's influence was a buried and forgotten heritage.

Even the name we use for the Messiah today—*Jesus*—was westernized to the point that Jews would not recognize it as coming from the Old Testament Scriptures. In Hebrew, the name we use for Him, *Jesus*, is actually the same as Joshua, the Hebrew leader who took over for Moses in the Old Testament. The name means "salvation," and Jews would pronounce it *Yeshua*. So that our Jewish brothers might recognize the name for who He truly is, you'll hear me and many other "One New Man" believers—a subject we'll discuss in the next chapter—use the name *Yeshua* instead of the Greek *Jesus*.

These divisions from Judaism would not only weaken the church but also foster destructive attitudes of anti-Semitism that would spread and fester in the centuries to follow. Jews would be blamed for the death of Christ, stereotyped as wealthy misers and swindlers, made scapegoats for a variety of negative circumstances, and sometimes killed or exiled, often by the very Christians who unknowingly shared their heritage.

Sometimes called "the longest hatred," antisemitism has persisted in many forms for over two thousand years. The racial antisemitism of the National Socialists (Nazis) took hatred of Jews to a genocidal extreme, yet the Holocaust began with words and ideas: stereotypes, sinister cartoons, and the gradual spread of hate.

In the first millennium of the Christian era, leaders in the

European Christian (Catholic) hierarchy developed or solidi-
fied as doctrine ideas that: all Jews were responsible for the
crucifixion of Christ; the destruction of the Temple by the
Romans and the scattering of the Jewish people was punishment both for past transgressions and for continued failure to
abandon their faith and accept Christianity.[10]

We don't have to look too far to see that anti-Semitism
has played a role in the history of the world, the church, and
our civilization. Its impact on economics, religion, literature,
entertainment—every aspect of our lives, in fact—has been
enormous and devastating. Consider this brief timeline, which
lists only a few examples out of countless many:

AD 240	Rome placed heavy taxation upon Jews—particularly farmers—for both revenue and supplies to fund continual military campaigns. Many were forced to flee the empire because they couldn't keep up with payments.
305	The Council of Elvira prohibited Christians in Spain from marrying or even sharing meals with Jews.
553	Byzantine emperor Justinian decreed that Jews could not read Hebrew books in their synagogues, and the Mishnah and other rabbinic commentaries were banned.
612	Spain's Visigoth king, Sisebut, issued the following decrees: • all debts to Jews were void, and • for Jews to be allowed to retain ownership of their land, they had to convert to Christianity. Within a year, he further declared that any unconverted Jews had to leave Spain. Some converted, were baptized, and remained, but many chose exile instead.[11]

1215	Pope Innocent III adopted four specific rules regarding Jews: • Jews must be identifiable in public via a mark on their clothing. • Jews could not collect interest when lending to Christians (they could lend but not profit), nor could they do business with Christians unless they obeyed church instruction. • Jews were not allowed to hold public office. • Jews converting to Christianity—for whatever reason—could no longer engage in Jewish observances.
1305	Pope Clement V was the first pope to threaten Jews with an economic boycott, attempting to force them into giving Christians no-interest loans.
1742	In December of that year, Empress Elizabeth of Russia expelled all Jews—thirty-five thousand in all—from her empire. When the senate said it would harm trade, she responded, "I don't desire any profits from the enemies of Christ." Among her deportees was her personal physician and commander of the army's medical branch, Antonio Ribera Sanchez.[12]
1933–1945	The Holocaust began in January of 1933, when Adolf Hitler became chancellor of Germany, and lasted until May of 1945, when Germany surrendered to the Allies. Persecution of Jews progressed from harassment and the smashing of shop windows to confinement in city ghettos to mass executions in concentration camps. The final death toll was approximately 6 million Jews, of which 1.5 million were children. Five thousand Jewish communities were destroyed. One-third of the world Jewish population died in these twelve years.[13]

AD 1972	On September 5, in the early morning, Palestinian terrorists stormed the Olympic Village apartment where the Israeli delegation to the Munich Olympics was staying. The terrorists killed two of the athletes before taking nine more hostage. Eventually, the terrorists took their captives to the Munich airport, where there was a shootout between the terrorists and West German police. By its end, the hostages, terrorists, and one policeman were dead. The Olympic games continued despite the tragedy.[14]

This list represents only a small sampling of anti-Semitism's sad history in the church and in the world. Unfortunately, it is a very real battle that many Jews still face. Anti-Semitism is alive and well today, spreading hatred of Israel throughout Arab nations and Europe. And even in the United States, there seems to be an uptick of anti-Jewish attitudes.

According to the Anti-Defamation League website: "From Jan. 1 to Sept. 30 [2017] there were 1,299 anti-Semitic incidents across the United States, including physical assaults, vandalism, and attacks on Jewish institutions. That total represents a 67 percent increase over the same period in 2016."[15] Many of these recorded incidents took place in schools—both K–12 and on college campuses. In 2016, 1,266 incidents were reported, which included "703 incidents of harassment, including 162 bomb threats against Jewish institutions; 584 incidents of vandalism, including 52 against Jewish institutions; [and] 12 physical assaults."[16] The incidents with the highest numbers of reports tended to be those with the largest Jewish populations: "New York State (267 incidents), California (197), Massachusetts (117), Florida (69), and Pennsylvania (58)."[17]

The distancing of the church from its Jewish roots over the

past two millennia has come at a high cost. It has bred silence that fed the development of anti-Semitism. It has caused us to miss important biblical truths because we interpreted Scripture throughout a Greco-Roman filter instead of reading it through the eyes of the culture that Jesus, the prophets, and the apostles were speaking to. And the persistence of replacement theology has undermined our relationship with the Creator by keeping us blind to the fulfillment of prophecy that is happening regularly right before our very eyes.

I believe that this blindness—whether it comes from ignorance, misinterpretation, or a desire to bury our heads in the sand—is particularly dangerous for us in the church today because it erodes our trust and prevents us from hearing what being open to God's calling can do. It's all too easy to let the combination of lies, disconnection, and confusion drive us into a reclusive posture where we feel we cannot trust anyone, even God. And if we allow our lives to come into such a highly defensive posture, we will never see the doors of opportunity before us, because our minds will be prisoners of our souls' distrust.

The Bible hints at this when it tells us,

> Hope deferred makes the heart sick,
> But when the desire comes, it is a tree of life.
>
> (PROVERBS 13:12)

You see, in order to walk at peace with our god, no matter what religion or god we follow, we must believe that this god is more powerful than we are, has a greater resource of wisdom and knowledge, and is going to speak to us in truth. There has to be faith and trust.

The biggest danger of replacement theology is that it puts Christians in a place where we cannot see or recognize crucial prophetic signs. In fact, we do not even know to look for them, and we have no idea where we fit into the picture.

Here's just one example of how replacement theology can plague the church with blindness regarding what God is doing in the world today. Scripture foretold what has happened with the nation of Israel since the Holocaust—from her statehood in 1948 and the reunification of Jerusalem in 1967 to current events like the US embassy moving to Jerusalem in 2018.

> Who has ever seen anything as strange as this?
> Who ever heard of such a thing?
> Has a nation ever been born in a single day?
> Has a country ever come forth in a mere moment?
> But by the time Jerusalem's birth pains begin,
> her children will be born.
>
> (ISAIAH 66:8 NLT)

And yet the vast majority of the church, misled by replacement theology, can't see this connection because they assume God abandoned the Jewish people long ago. As a result they miss both the prophetic significance and the promise of hope in present-day Israel.

So many of the prophecies surrounding Israel could only be fulfilled by a people and nation of Israel. When we cling to the misunderstanding that the church replaces Israel under the new covenant, we will miss the miraculous, faithful hand of God. We will not see how faithfully He fulfills His promises in the world today, and so we will struggle to trust Him.

Adherents of replacement theology do not recognize the Jews as still being God's chosen people nor Israel as God's chosen nation. They don't understand that the new covenant does not nullify the older covenants. So they have difficulty believing that

the land of Israel is part of God's future plan or recognizing it
as the central player in the book of Revelation and other eschato-
logical prophecies. Instead, they are stuck with believing that the
church only receives all such blessings spiritually, as a type and
shadow of what Israel should have been.

And while I do believe that we have been grafted into the promises of God and that there is a spiritual transfer and application for
our lives as believers, I do not believe in any way that the church has
taken the place of Israel or that God is done with the Jewish people.
If that were the case—if God had broken covenant with the Jews,
who are our roots—how could we put our trust in His faithfulness
to us as the branches? How can we trust a God who disregarded
His own covenant people and replaced them? Who trusts a Father
like that?

Other ministers have come to the same conclusions. For
example, Derek Prince stated in his book *The Destiny of Israel and
the Church*:

> Essential truth is usually simple, and the truth is, Israel is
> Israel, and the Church is the Church. . . . Up to this point, we
> have been considering Israel and the Church as if they were
> two separate entities, but this is not really accurate.[18]

I agree wholeheartedly. The Jewish people and the Christian
church share too much to be considered separately. For we are both
heirs of the covenantal relationship God made with Abraham:

> I will bless those who bless you,
> And I will curse him who curses you;
> And in you all the families of the earth shall be blessed.
>
> (GENESIS 12:3)

When God desired to restore His covenant with humanity—the covenant that had been broken at Eden—He restored it through Abraham, the first Jew, who became the father of many nations. Therefore, when we separate from the customs, traditions, and understandings of our roots, we lose touch with our true and full inheritance, the rich blessings that can be ours because of God's promises to the seed of Abraham.

Because God's covenants with the Jews have never been nullified, and because they are part of our heritage as followers of Yeshua, these blessings are intimately linked to an understanding of the place of Israel and the role of the Jewish people both in history and in our future. With Israel and the Jewish people replaced, missing, substituted, forgotten, or removed as a piece on God's prophetic chessboard, we are robbed of the spiritual fullness that comes when we reconnect with our forgotten heritage. As the apostle Paul wrote: "Now if [Israel's] fall is riches for the world, and their failure riches for the Gentiles, how much more their fullness!" (Romans 11:12).

When we are in agreement with a lie, we are enslaved to the lie. But when we are in covenant with the truth, we are empowered by the truth. And this empowerment can be ours when we reject replacement theology and centuries of misunderstanding and embrace the Jewish part of our Christian heritage.

When we understand the history of the disconnection of the church from her Jewish roots, we are better equipped for God's reconnection. We are more open to His revelation and experience a new hunger for His Word. This creates new depths of understanding and a firmer place for us to stand as part of His kingdom. And I'm telling you from experience, when Jew and Gentile come together to do the will of God, that's where the real adventure begins.

thirteen

ONE NEW MAN

> *For He Himself is our peace, who has made both one,*
> *and has broken down the middle wall of separation,*
> *having abolished in His flesh the enmity, that is, the*
> *law of commandments contained in ordinances, so as*
> *to create in Himself one new man from the two, thus*
> *making peace, and that He might reconcile them both*
> *to God in one body through the cross, thereby putting*
> *to death the enmity.*
>
> —EPHESIANS 2:14–16

IN EPHESIANS 2:14–16, quoted at the beginning of this chapter, Paul described how God tore down the wall of separation between Jew and Gentile to create "one new man, thus making peace" between us and reconciling us together to Himself. This is another reason why enmity toward the Jews—or any other ethnic group, for that matter—is counter to Scripture and to

God's intent of sending His Son to reconcile the world back to Himself. The power of God is not experienced in division, but in His divine unity.

Beginning with the early church—and even before—we've seen special things happen when Jew and Gentile have come together. Ruth, who was a Moabite, married Boaz, who was Jewish, and their descendants gave birth to King David—plus, Ruth never would have married Boaz had she not stayed close to her Jewish mother-in-law, Naomi. There are some who believe that Caleb, who did great things with Joshua, had a Gentile background. And look at what happened when Peter went to the house of Cornelius and his band of Italian soldiers, and then throughout the rest of the book of Acts when Paul, Barnabas, and Silas went to the Gentile nations and then all the way to Rome. These are all biblical examples of Jews and Gentiles operating together spiritually as One New Man.

We can see other examples throughout history: Christopher Columbus, who is believed to have been Jewish because his diary was written in Hebrew, worked together with a Spanish crew to travel to the New World. Haym Salomon, a Jewish lender, helped finance George Washington's army. Generations later, Abraham Lincoln enlisted Abraham Jonas, another Jewish man, as a legal and political associate and advisor. The two became close friends and together helped save the United States from being torn in two.

Often when God brings Jews and Gentiles together, there is a profound historic shift. The same can be said of Gentiles like Oskar Schindler and Corrie ten Boom, who helped the Jews during the Holocaust. And had not Gentiles joined in supporting the Jews following the Holocaust, the nation of modern Israel might never have been born—which is, of course, the most prophetic event of the last century.

When Jews and Gentiles labor together, there is a profound

shift not only in the natural but also in the spirit. You might have heard of the Brownsville revival that swept Pensacola, Florida, beginning in 1995. Its leadership included Pastor John Kilpatrick, a man of Cherokee roots, as well as Dick Reuben and Michael Brown, who are both Jewish. Steve Hill came to the revival as an evangelist, preaching repentance like John the Baptist. You can see the pattern: John Kilpatrick, *First* Nations; Dick Reuben and Michael Brown, *first*born Jews; Steve Hill, *first*fruit Gentile.[1] Their covenant agreement created a three-stranded cord of alignment that ushered in one of the largest revivals in recent history.

This pattern is unmistakable. When you see God assembling leaders from various Gentile ethnicities together with the Jewish people, it would be wise to get ready for a sovereign move!

Blessings are always more accessible to us when we know and understand God's ways. For me, it always comes back to things I can invest: talents, treasure (money), or especially time. One of the questions that I often ask myself, for example, is "How did I get into this journey of seeking to be in synergy with God's timing?"

As a young businessman, I learned the valuable lesson that timing is everything. And now, as a student of Bible prophecy, I can easily see that everything flows historically and prophetically according to God's created forces operating in agreement with His calendar—the lunar calendar of the Jews, punctuated with feasts and holy days that commemorate His covenant relationship with His people, builds a rhythm of repentance and renewal into our days and months and years. These biblical feasts include Passover, Shavuot (Pentecost), and Sukkot (the Feast of Tabernacles). All three of these feasts are pilgrim feasts where Jewish men were required to journey from their homes and bring an offering to Jerusalem.

Scripture records some of the times when Jesus and His disciples honored these feasts. For example, Jesus said this of Passover on the night He was betrayed: "With fervent desire I have desired to eat this Passover with you before I suffer" (Luke 22:15).

It's important to remember that early Christians of the first three centuries had no Easter. That holiday was a Roman addition. Instead of Easter, the earliest believers would have celebrated Passover as a dual celebration—remembering Israel's deliverance from Egypt and also the week of Christ's Passion, culminating in His death, burial, and resurrection.

We also see Jesus and His disciples attending Sukkot, the Feast of Tabernacles:

> Now the Jews' Feast of the Tabernacles was at hand. . . . He also went up to the feast, not openly, but as it were in secret. Then the Jews sought Him at the feast, and said, "Where is He?" And there was much complaining among the people concerning Him. Some said, "He is good"; others said, "No, on the contrary, He deceives the people." However, no one spoke openly of Him for fear of the Jews. Now about the middle of the feast Jesus went up into the temple and taught. (John 7:2, 10–14)

It should also be noted that the dramatic events of Pentecost happened while men and women were gathered in Jerusalem for Shavuot, which is the memorial celebration of the giving of the Torah and is celebrated fifty days after Passover. They did not just happen to be in Jerusalem for the visitation of the Holy Spirit. They were in the right place at the right time because they were in touch with their cultural and spiritual roots.

> When the Day of Pentecost had fully come, they were all with one accord in one place. . . . And there were dwelling in Jerusalem Jews, devout men, from every nation under heaven. (Acts 2:1, 5)

I list these Scriptures simply to establish the fact that Jesus
and His disciples honored the feasts of the Lord during His lifetime. His disciples continued in these observances even after His
ascension, as we see in the first chapters of Acts. There is so much
richness and revelation in the days that our Lord has set aside as
moeds (translated as "feasts" in the Bible but it's more accurately
translated as "divine appointments") that I can only scratch the
surface in this chapter. But I can say that, for us, the revelation has
been transformative—life changing.

Over the last twenty-six years, my family, along with many
members of House of David and partners of Curt Landry
Ministries, have experienced life-changing blessings from adjust-
ing our lives to honor the biblical calendar. We make it a priority
to observe the Jewish holy days, which the Old Testament calls
"feasts of the LORD" (Leviticus 23:2, for example). And I would
attribute many of God's blessings in our lives to adopting these
principles and putting God's calendar and ways above our own
agendas and schedules.

When God first planted in me the desire to follow His calendar and His ways, I jokingly said, "He tricked me," because it was
not a revelation of potential blessings that birthed this quest but
rather an emotion that pierced my heart and opened my soul to
new possibilities of worship. It brought me right back to Matthew
6:33, but now in its fullness: "But seek first the kingdom of God
and His righteousness, and all these things shall be added to you."

When Christie and I began ordering our lives around God's
calendar, we made a point of combining a Jewish awareness with
our Gentile culture, and we found that good things tended to happen as a result. Now all our ministries and our business operate
according to this principle, with a heart to honor God and to do
things in alignment with His ways and His structured plan. I will
be the first to admit that this is not easy. Keeping God's calendar

can be very disruptive when paired with our modern Gregorian[2] calendar and all the events in our lives. Over the years my family and I have had to say no to many good things because of our commitment to honor the Lord's way of doing things.

However, our personal experience in doing this has taught us that honor is the currency of heaven. Christie and I have been so blessed to see that Megann and Paul have not had to struggle with some of the issues we walked through, and I believe this freedom will be even more evident in my granddaughter Ariebella's life as she carries my family's third generation in covenant with God. I am convinced that much of the favor my children and granddaughter now walk in is due in part to living in sync with God's calendar.

Every year now, for instance, we have more than five hundred people travel to the House of David from around the world for a full sit-down *seder*[3] meal at Passover. Thousands more participate online. This raises the question: Why would someone travel from Africa or Singapore all the way to the middle of nowhere in Oklahoma (where we now live) for a four-hour service? Psalm 23:5 suggests an answer:

> You prepare a table before me in the presence of my enemies;
> You anoint my head with oil;
> My cup runs over.

The table and the cup mentioned in Psalm 23 can be related to the Passover table. Passover offers nine blessings that cover every aspect of life. These are listed in Exodus 23:20–33, which contains God's instructions to Moses before the first Passover in Egypt.

1. *Divine protection:* "Behold, I send an Angel before you to keep you in the way and to bring you into the place which I have prepared" (v. 20).

2. *Protection from enemies through positioning and alignment:*
   "But if you indeed obey His voice and do all that I speak,
   then I will be an enemy to your enemies and an adversary
   to your adversaries" (v. 22).

3. *Commissioning of divine authority:* "You shall not bow
   down to their gods, nor serve them, nor do according to
   their works; but you shall utterly overthrow them and
   completely break down their sacred pillars" (v. 24).

4. *Supernatural health and kingdom prosperity:* "So you shall
   serve the LORD your God, and He will bless your bread
   and your water. And I will take sickness away from the
   midst of you" (v. 25).

5. *Covenant protection for multiplication and longevity:* "No one
   shall suffer miscarriage or be barren in your land; I will
   fulfill the number of your days" (v. 26).

6. *A godly release of fear and respect from enemies:* "I will send
   My fear before you, I will cause confusion among all the
   people to whom you come, and will make all your enemies turn their backs to you" (v. 27).

7. *Relief from the threat of enemies:* "And I will send hornets
   before you, which shall drive out the Hivite, the Canaanite,
   and the Hittite from before you" (v. 28).

8. *The gift of dominion and an increased inheritance:* "Little by
   little I will drive them out from before you, until you have
   increased, and you inherit the land" (v. 30).

9. *Freedom from corrupt covenants:* "They shall not dwell in
   your land, lest they make you sin against Me. For if you
   serve their gods, it will surely be a snare to you" (v. 33).

It is my belief that these blessings are activated when we slide
our feet under the Father's table at Passover. As a family, we have
decreed these blessings over our hearts, our lives, our finances,

our health, and our homes every year for the past twenty-six years—and we continue to see them manifest.

For Christians, of course, the *seder* meal carries an added depth of meaning. On the night that He was betrayed, Yeshua consecrated the last *seder* meal He would share with His disciples. It was from this passage that the Lord's Table or Holy Communion was instituted:

> When the hour had come, He sat down, and the twelve apostles with Him. Then He said to them, "With fervent desire I have desired to eat this Passover with you before I suffer; for I say to you, I will no longer eat of it until it is fulfilled in the kingdom of God."
>
> Then He took the cup, and gave thanks, and said, "Take this and divide it among yourselves; for I say to you, I will not drink of the fruit of the vine until the kingdom of God comes."
>
> And He took bread, gave thanks and broke it, and gave it to them, saying, "This is My body which is given for you; do this in remembrance of Me." (Luke 22:14–19)

Notice the combination of covenant meal with covenant celebration in this passage. When Jesus said, "Do this in remembrance of Me," He was sitting at a Passover *seder* table with His Jewish disciples, partaking of a meal and an observance they would have experienced every year of their lives. He was clearly telling His disciples that they should remember Him when they broke bread at future *seder* tables. He was speaking to a Jewish audience who had cultural understanding of their roots.

The church, on the other hand, has broken down the observance of communion to the point that we've almost forgotten the first sharing of bread and wine, body and blood, happened at the Passover table. "Do this in remembrance of Me" refers strictly to the breaking of bread and the sipping of wine or juice. We don't even practice this as part of a festive meal together. Instead, we tend to shroud it in ominousness and detach it as much as possible from any real interaction—true communion—with one another. While the table may be prepared, we, the guests, are more or less absent.

This cultural confusion keeps us from coming to His table as we should, which is yet another reason the church needs to reconnect to our roots. We need to learn how to properly show up at the Father's table. That is the only way for His life—the life that comes up from the roots—to flow into us afresh.

There is a great richness in the practice of communion, but so much more richness is available to us—a full *seder* table of inheritance. In fact, Passover is a good place to start in understanding the rhythm of remembrances that is the cycle of Jewish feasts. Each has a special meaning and rituals aimed at reminding us of the covenants and our parts in them.

In a proper Passover *seder,* for example, there are four cups served, not just one. They represent four further blessings that the Jews were to remember each time they drank from them. These represent four aspects of the deliverance from Egypt that the Jews experienced in the first Passover. The four cups are:

1. *The cup of sanctification:* This cup represents holiness and the cleansing we need to be able to receive from the Lord.
2. *The cup of plagues:* This cup reminds us of the deliverance of the plagues of Egypt, but it also represents healing from sickness and disease.
3. *The cup of redemption:* Yeshua was holding this cup when He said, "Do this in remembrance of Me"—thus decreeing that He was the Passover Lamb who would redeem His people and the world. Three years earlier, when Yeshua

came to be baptized by John the Baptist, John had proclaimed by the Spirit, "Behold! The Lamb of God who takes away the sin of the world!" (John 1:29). So when Jesus now said, "Do this in remembrance of Me," He was not cancelling Passover, but embracing it. Because this was the Passover, He empowered the cup of redemption as only the Messiah could do—by His soon coming death on the cross and resurrection from the grave.

4. *The cup of praise:* I believe this is the cup we will receive from Yeshua Himself as we enter into heaven. He will hand us a wedding cup (or "Kiddush cup") and say, "Well done, good and faithful servant." It is important to understand that in a Jewish wedding, the groom extends this cup to the bride, and she drinks from it as a sign of her acceptance of the covenant being offered. Her acceptance of the cup seals the marriage.

To the Jews, Passover signifies a new beginning and is a preparation feast for consecration. It is also the beginning of the Feast of Unleavened Bread (or Chag HaMatzot), a time where we focus on the removal of leaven—which represents sin—from our lives. Just as we take the yeast out of our homes, we also try to remove anything in our lives that might cause pride or allow arrogance to arise. Passover also marks the beginning of a fifty-day period before Shavuot, a time of anticipation and preparation. The practice of marking these days is referred to as the "counting of the Omer."

Shavuot, which coincides with Pentecost, commemorates the impartation of instruction when Moses received the law. To Jews, it is the birthday of the Torah. For Christians, of course, Pentecost also marks the birthday of the church, the time when the Holy Spirit filled and empowered the New Testament church. Fire is an integral part of both celebrations. Just as fire burned God's instruction onto the stones of Moses, the Holy Spirit burned His baptism into the hearts of the disciples in the Upper Room.

In these three spring feasts—Passover, Unleavened Bread, and Shavuot—we can see a pattern established by God of cleansing and empowerment. The same pattern shows itself in the fall feasts, beginning with Rosh Hashanah, a two-day observance also known as the Feast of Trumpets, so named for the practice of blowing a ram's horn called a *shofar*. Rosh Hashanah marks the beginning of the civil Jewish New Year. The blowing of the shofar is a blast to awaken the people to examine their lives and hearts and align themselves with God's ways for the next year.

Rosh Hashanah also begins a ten-day period of introspection called the High Holy Days, or the Days of Awe. These ten days end with the observance of Yom Kippur, or Day of Atonement, considered the most solemn day of the year. Yom Kippur is a memorial fast that focuses on sin and repentance and reminds us that God always makes a scapegoat available for our sin, should we choose to receive it, as He cleanses us in preparation for the year ahead. For Christian believers, this is a time where we consciously bring everything in our lives under the blood of Yeshua.

Sukkot, the Feast of Tabernacles, also called the Feast of Booths, is a fall harvest festival celebrated in the spirit of an wedding celebration. For eight days, meals and celebrations are held outdoors in a temporary structure called a *sukkah*—usually a three-sided dwelling whose roof has an opening large enough to look out and see the stars. The *sukkah*, reminiscent of the tents where the Israelites slept in the wilderness, is intended to remind us that in God alone we find our shelter and provision. When we see the stars of the sky through the roof of the *sukkah*, we are reminded of God's covenant promise to Abraham that his descendants would be as numerous as the stars. For Christians, this festival marks an annual recommitment of trusting the Lord in a relational way as the husband of the church. To do so, we remember Jesus' parable of the wise virgins who had their lamps filled and their wicks trimmed while waiting for the coming of the bridegroom (Matthew 25:1–13).

Each feast (or fast) in the Jewish calendar has its associated customs, instructions, offerings, and blessings that are rooted in the great heritage of our faith. They are excellent reminders and spiritual traditions to keep us in alignment with God's heart and the ways He established in His Word. Honoring the feasts of the Lord is a great way for families to discipline their thoughts together and remember to put God first in all things. This spiritual rhythm helps us stay in step with God's covenant with us and the ways it unfolds according to His appointed timetable.

But the feasts of the Lord are not just history and instruction.[4] They have a very real modern-day application that was established to protect us and our families by creating memories together and giving every member a place at the table to worship God. When we read in Leviticus 23 that we are to do this "throughout [our] generations" (vv. 14, 21, 31, 41), that word *generations* represents "families"—your family, my family, and all the families of the church together.

The enemy is doing all he can to destroy the family unit, as evidenced by everything from skyrocketing divorce rates to the sexual identity crisis happening around the world today. He is using every channel he can to dismantle the family at its core and distort the family identity. The church has fallen into his trap and unknowingly separated itself from many of God's blessings because we've disconnected from and forgotten our true heritage. When we pull away from God's instruction and from our Father's table, we open the door of our lives to the enemy and unnecessary spiritual warfare.

Malachi, whose name meant "my messenger," was a prophet in the days of Nehemiah, and his message was spoken to a generation that was full of corruption—dishonorable priests, marital infidelity, hypocrisy, and false worship. The prophet brought a strong word of correction, and then God's prophets fell silent until Yeshua came, a period of four hundred years. Thus Malachi was the last signpost pointing to the coming of the Messiah.

> But who can endure the day of His coming?
> And who can stand when He appears?
> For He is like a refiner's fire
> And like launderers' soap.
> He will sit as a refiner and a purifier of silver;
> He will purify the sons of Levi,
> And purge them as gold and silver,
> That they may offer to the LORD
> An offering in righteousness.
> Then the offering of Judah and Jerusalem
> Will be pleasant to the LORD,
> As in the days of old,
> As in former years.
>
>   (MALACHI 3:2–4)

Note that even in this forward-looking prophecy, Malachi spoke of the practice of offerings to be given on traditional feast days "as in the days of old." Thus He affirms the blessing of walking in rhythm with God's season and instruction, even after the Messiah has come.

When the fourth-century councils severed us from the roots of our faith and from observance of the Jewish feasts, we were also separated from the blessings poured out when walking in rhythm with God's seasons and instruction. In the process, I believe, we lost something intrinsic to our very identity. There is an internal clock within each individual that keeps us in synergy with God's timetables. It's when we get out of sync with that clock that we begin to lose ourselves.

Christie and I have found that when we returned to our heritage and began following His instruction, we experienced the kind of abundant blessings described in Malachi 3:10–11:

> "Bring all the tithes into the storehouse so there will be enough food in my Temple. If you do," says the LORD of Heaven's Armies, "I will open the windows of heaven for you. I will pour out a blessing so great you won't have enough room to take it in! Try it! Put me to the test! Your crops will be abundant, for I will guard them from insects and disease. Your grapes will not fall from the vine before they are ripe," says the LORD of Heaven's Armies. (NLT)

Malachi's words here, of course, refer to financial matters—the blessings that come to us when we give back to the Lord. And Christie and I found this to be true since we began the practice not only of tithing but also of giving offerings at God's appointed feasts. This practice has strengthened our sense of identity and helped us connect with our purpose. It has also proven to be a great teaching tool of legacy and discipline as we witness God's faithfulness to provide.

Malachi's blessings ultimately were not about money, but about the restoration of families. What is abundant wealth if you do not have peace in your homes and your relationships? Malachi spoke his words of warning as an invitation to obedience that ended with the hope of family restoration, when "the hearts of fathers [will turn] to their children, and the hearts of children to their fathers" (Malachi 4:6).

The silence that followed Malachi's prophecies came because the words of God that were spoken through His prophets were not heeded. They fell on deaf ears as God's people broke covenant with Him and with one another. Subsequently families continued to fall apart, separated from the blessing and the goodness of the Father. When the children do not see the evidence of the blessing of God in their parents' lives, confusion and contempt inevitably follow.

In that light, Malachi was not just speaking a word for that day, but one for today as well. Malachi 3:1 speaks of the generation that would see the Lord return "suddenly."

> "Behold, I send My messenger,
> And he will prepare the way before Me.
> And the Lord, whom you seek,
> Will *suddenly* come to His temple,
> Even the Messenger of the covenant,
> In whom you delight.
> Behold, He is coming,"
> Says the LORD of hosts.
>
> (MALACHI 3:1)

There was nothing sudden about Yeshua's first coming as a child born to Mary. The "suddenly" message was for our generation and is an introduction to Ephesians 2 and the reunifying message of the One New Man.

The true Messenger of the covenant is returning. He is coming, and this time He really will come suddenly—so we must be ready:

> Watch therefore, for you do not know what hour your Lord
> is coming. But know this, that if the master of the house

had known what hour the thief would come, he would have watched and not allowed his house to be broken into. Therefore you also be ready, for the Son of Man is coming at an hour you do not expect. (Matthew 24:42–44)

These are the things God is emphasizing for this generation—one that will likely see His sudden appearance. Are Jew and Gentile standing together ready for His return? Are our homes and families in order, understanding the full and true heritage of what it means to make Yeshua their Lord and Savior? Are we doing God's things God's ways? Are we in sync with His time-tables? Are our lamps trimmed and full, ready for the coming of the Bridegroom?

When Yeshua returns, will we be as one, chasing His dreams together—Jew and Gentile, parent and child, generation and generation, walking in the fullness of both covenants? Are we ready to embrace His callings for such a time as this?

If we're going to be, we need to learn to walk in His faith, His peace (*shalom*), and His multiplication power.

fourteen

FAITH

*Nevertheless, when the Son of Man comes, will He
really find faith on the earth?*

—Luke 18:8

WHEN MEGANN WAS ABOUT FOUR or five years old,
my adoptive dad, Ray, had a heart attack. At the time he lived
in Portland, Oregon, and was in a serious relationship. My adoptive mother, Rita, had passed away years earlier, when I was only
twenty-two. Portland was only about a four-hour drive from us
in Washington, so when Ray's fiancée called me with the news, I
told her, "We'll be right there." As quickly as we could, we got in
the car and were on our way.

This was in the mid-1990s, so I had only been saved a few
years, but in that time I had learned a few things about prayer
and hearing the voice of God. So I prayed about my dad as I
drove. And as we got near the Columbia River to cross over into

Portland, God told me, *"I want you to lay hands on him, and I'm going to heal him."*

Now, that might seem a bit over the top, but something strange had been happening to me back at our church in Washington. It was embarrassing, in fact. Christie and I weren't in ministry yet, just members of the church. But when they called the elders of the church down front to pray for people who had needs according to James 5:13–15, the people with needs would line up where Christie and I were instead. They wanted me to pray for them because they had heard that God healed people when I prayed for them.

The whole thing was a little awkward. I wasn't an elder, and I wasn't even in the front of the sanctuary as someone called to pray for others, but here they came all the same. It got me in a bit of trouble with the elders at first. But I told them, "Listen, it's not my fault. I'm not putting up a sign or anything calling people to 'Come over here.' I actually try to ignore them and shoo them to the front. I don't even make eye contact." The elders eventually recognized God at work, though, and they knew enough to let Him do as He saw fit.

In the years to follow, I would come to realize that this gift for healing was a gifting of the Holy Spirit on my life. I eventually ministered with T. L. Osborn, who ran large crusades around the world where incredible miracles happened. He once told me, "You're the only person I ever met who has the gift of miracles and the gift of faith. You'll see one or the other, but I've rarely seen the two together. Young man, that gives you a lot of responsibility for the kingdom."

So when God told me He was going to heal my dad, I'd already had a little experience in seeing God do that. I just wondered how I was going to get him alone to lay hands on him and pray without being interrupted. As it turned out, God had that well in hand already.

We went into Dad's room bearing balloons and get-well cards, probably looking something like a circus procession. And Dad, who was always very reserved, blurted out, "It's great to see everybody!" He was especially happy that his grandbaby was there—he loved Megann. We sat her on the edge of his bed for a bit and visited.

Then after a little while he said, "I'm really tired. I don't want to be rude, but can I spend some time alone with Curtis?"

Everyone said yes, then left to get something to eat. Now remember, my father Ray was a marine and as tough as they come. You know how kids say, "My dad can beat up your dad"? Most kids just said that, but if I said it, it was for real, and everyone knew it.

No one messed with Ray. He'd always been the big, square-jawed boxer guy with giant hands and thick wrists. So it was tough to see him in bed, weak and pale.

I didn't know what to say, so we just sat together while he rested. Then he said, "You know, I'm not religious like you, I'll tell you."

He knew some of the story I've already shared here and was aware that church had become a central part of my life. He knew about us being in a group that spent millions to fly Jews from Russia to Israel. He also knew about my work selling fruit and was keenly aware that God was prospering us.

The first time he'd visited our home in Washington, in fact, he'd asked, "How many families live in this?"

"Just Christie, Megann, and I," I told him.

He shook his head. "Well, why in the world do you need this much space?"

"This is what I want to live in, Dad."

"Well, it seems like a waste of money to me."

That was just who he was, where he came from. He couldn't wrap his mind around our lives, and he didn't mind telling us so.

But now, sitting there in the hospital, all that bluster was gone. He looked at me seriously and asked, "Where do you get this faith?"

I said, "Well, part of it's your fault."

"My fault?" He shook his head. "I told you—I'm not religious."

"Yeah," I replied, "but when people become Christians, their first impressions of God the Father tend to reflect their earthly fathers. And a lot of people struggle with this because they don't have good memories of their earthly fathers. They have a hard time removing the limitations of their earthly experience when stepping to connect with the divine."

"All right," he said, "but what does that have to do with me?"

I sat looking at him for a minute, and then I told him, "Because you said, 'We're going to get a swing set, and it's going to come on Thursday.' No one else in the neighborhood had anything like that, but you said we were going to get one.

"I remember being on the playground at St. Jerome's looking up La Tijeras Boulevard and seeing a truck. It had all this stuff on the back, but I could make out what looked like a fort. And the instant I saw it, I knew that truck was going to our house. After school, I ran a hundred miles an hour from there to our house because I wanted to play on that swing set."

I paused, then looked up at him. "You said that it would happen and that it would happen on such and such a day, and it happened just like you said it would. You always delivered. You were always home at five o'clock. When Mom said, 'Wait until your father gets home,' we knew we were going to get it and that you'd be home at five o'clock to give it to us."

I looked at my hands. "I'm in business now, and I know what it means to have a job and responsibilities and obligations. I know how work stuff can seem more urgent and important than being home at five o'clock with your family. But you never wavered.

You were consistent. When you said something was going to happen, when you made a promise, I knew it was going to happen.

"I take that consistency to my relationship with my heavenly Father. I know how to trust in Him, because you left a good pattern. I've ministered to enough people in deliverance and healing to know how fortunate I was to have that consistency in my life. I'll always honor you for that."

I looked up and saw he had tears in his eyes. "Wow," he said, "I didn't know that."

"You needed to know it," I told him.

At that moment, I knew God was making room for me to pray for him, but I still didn't know how. It wasn't like I was going to jump up and say, "Okay now, Dad, I'm going to lay hands on you, and God is going to heal you." I knew he wouldn't understand that.

He looked at me and said, "I've got a really strange request for you."

"Okay."

"Listen, I can't sleep in this place." He paused. "And to be honest with you, I'm scared. I'm not ready to die." He looked into my eyes. "I'm not like you."

"Okay," I said again.

"I need to go to sleep. And you have so much faith in your God, I feel like if I could just hold your hand and go to sleep, I'll be okay."

I smiled, nodded, and took his hand. That was it. I was laying hands on him. Nothing elaborate, just that big, gnarly hand in my hand. I prayed in my heart quietly; I didn't pray out loud. And he fell asleep. A little while later I left.

That night my dad had another heart attack, and it caused what the doctors call a Mother Nature bypass. It blew out the blockage that had caused his first heart attack. The doctors considered it a freak accident, but I knew it was a miracle, and so did my dad.

He left the hospital the next day.

A lot of people would have tried to take advantage of my dad's fear and weakness to lead him to the Lord right then and there, but I knew better. If I had done that, it would not have been on his terms and motivated by panic, not faith. Besides, I knew my Father was going to heal my father because He had already told me He would.

About a month later I did lead Dad to the Lord, though, and on his terms. There was no emotional manipulation, and his decision was his own. He lived another twenty-some years after that.

I can't think of any situation I've been in—even when the miracles were bigger—that gives a better example of how faith works. It's a covenant act: we do the small thing, while God does the big thing.

Think of Abraham going up the hill with Isaac to sacrifice him. He did it knowing that Isaac was going to come back down with him somehow, because Isaac was the son of promise. Abraham knew the power of that promise and concluded "that God was able to raise him up, even from the dead, from which he also received him in a figurative sense" (Hebrews 11:19). Faith is simply a matter of trust, one you know you can stake your life on—or that of your loved ones.

Our carnal minds and soulish natures long for, look for, and seek after evidence and facts to help us make quality decisions. But seeking the Father's kingdom first requires a disciplined walk of faith that is grown and exercised in practice before it becomes something we can regularly rely on. The test, so to speak, is not in our desire to walk in Matthew 6:33, but in our ability to rest in and obey Matthew 6:34: "Therefore do not worry about tomorrow, for tomorrow will worry about its own things. Sufficient for the day is its own trouble."

This practice of walking by faith while listening to and being led by the Holy Spirit must be driven by love and passion for the Father because faith works through love. Love and faith are spiritual forces that together hold the power and anointing to break the yokes of bondage and all the powers of darkness. It is a daily exercise where we learn to see ourselves as victorious and to praise God in advance of what we are trusting to see happen. We must believe in God's faithfulness for the manifestation, trusting that He is sovereign over all things and has all well in hand.

To the Hebraic mind, believing God is the key to faith. It is trusting in His very existence as evidence that He will do what He says. When Moses asked for what he would tell the children of Israel in Egypt when he went to deliver them,

> God said to Moses, "I AM WHO I AM." And He said, "Thus you shall say to the children of Israel, 'I AM has sent me to you.'" Moreover God said to Moses, "Thus you shall say to the children of Israel: 'The LORD God of your fathers, the God of Abraham, the God of Isaac, and the God of Jacob, has sent me to you. This is My name forever, and this is My memorial to all generations.'" (Exodus 3:14–15)

Hebrews 11:6, which we've looked at several times before, reflects the same understanding: "Without faith it is impossible to please Him, for he who comes to God must believe that He is, and that He is a rewarder of those who diligently seek Him."

This faith, which has a sense of standing strong in times of trial, is based in trusting in the steadfastness and immutability of the God who is.

Emunah, the Hebrew word for all this, can be loosely translated as "faithfulness." According to *Strong's Concordance* it also implies "firmness, steadfastness, and fidelity"[1] and is rooted in the word *aman,* which means to believe, confirm, or support.[2] *Vine's Complete Expository Dictionary of Old and New Testament Words* tells us that *emunah* means "firmness; faithfulness; truth; honesty; official obligation."[3]

Emunah is a state of mind, a discipline. It means to stand like a soldier who won't leave his post, will hold the line, won't give up an inch to the enemy, and has complete confidence in God's protection.

> Therefore take up the whole armor of God, that you may be able to withstand in the evil day, and having done all, to stand. Stand therefore. (Ephesians 6:13–14)

The Scriptures even tell us that "the just shall live by . . . faith [*emunah*]" (Habakkuk 2:4; see also Romans 1:17, Galatians 3:11, and Hebrews 10:38). For in it the righteousness of God is revealed from faith to faith; as it is written, "The just shall live by faith" (Romans 1:17).

Rabbi Tzvi Freeman wrote this of *emunah,* which is generally translated simply as "faith" but one that involves so much more than belief:

> We're used to thinking of faith as a strategy for people who can't think for themselves. "The fool believes everything," Solomon writes, "the wise man understands." Emunah, however, is an innate conviction, a perception of truth that transcends, rather than evades, reason. Quite the contrary, wisdom, understanding and knowledge can further enhance true emunah.
>
> Nevertheless, emunah is not based on reason. Reason can never attain the certainty of emunah, since, reasonably speaking, a greater reasoning might always come along and prove your reasons wrong. In this way, emunah is similar

to seeing first hand: Reason can help you better understand what you see, but it will have a hard time convincing you that you never saw it. So too, emunah endures even when reason can't catch up.[4]

While a person may use faith to avoid reason (or because he or she is incapable of reason), this is not really faith, but simply avoidance. This person is simply borrowing the belief of others. When a person has profound *emunah* about a truth, however, it is not so much something decided on as it is "part and parcel of his very own essence and being."[5]

The greatest test of this, according to Rabbi Freeman, would then be martyrdom. A person won't die for what other people believe, only for something he or she is truly, soulishly convinced is truer than life itself. This is not a subrational decision, but super-rational, and "a person with super-rational emunah sees no choice—to deny his emunah is to deny the quintessence of his being."[6]

Taken in the context of *emunah*, faith is not just a muscle to be exercised and increased but a trustworthy covenant foundation in which to hope.

Faith is the substance of things hoped for, the evidence of things not seen. (Hebrews 11:1)

My ministry partners and I have seen this in so many of the endeavors God has put into our hearts. Our *emunah* is the evidence that the things God has shown us and sown into our hearts are trustworthy and that when we apply our hand to the plow with His, they will come to pass.

For faith to work this way, however, we do need vision. Faith, trust, and vision are all necessary components of an empowered life, a three-stranded cord of truth. And vision is especially important in a high-level faith walk.

> Where there is no vision, the people perish: but he that keepeth
> the law, happy is he. (Proverbs 29:18 KJV)

The vision referenced in this verse is clearly one from God, not just something we imagine on our own. The New King James Version translates the same word as "revelation," the English Standard Version translates it as "prophetic vision."

God's vision, the revelation of God's vision, and the work He has for your life will always line up with His Word—His law. Remember that the Hebrew word for law is *torah*, which translates as "direction or instruction." So God's vision for our lives will always be in alignment with His biblical instruction, hidden in His Word. His Word created us, and His Word will also direct us, providing that we seek it.

In 1996, Christie and I moved from Washington to Arkansas, living on the border of Arkansas and Oklahoma. Then in 1997 or 1998, a few years after we left the apple business and were actively seeking the Lord for direction on the ministry, we felt we were called to build. We officially moved back to Oklahoma in 2002 to begin the ministry.

While seeking direction about the ministry, the Lord clearly spoke to us that we were to fast and pray for three days. We were joined by a few other intercessors at a secluded house in the woods of northeast Oklahoma.

On the third and final day of this assignment, I had a vision of a gigantic baby, complete with diaper, suspended in the air before me. It looked as big as a refrigerator!

As I gazed at this vision in amazement, I asked the Lord, "What am I looking at?"

He said, *"You are looking at your future ministry."*

"But why is the baby so large?"

God impressed upon me that I was seeing the baby as huge so that I would not make the mistake of thinking that one person alone could handle its care and feeding. Nurturing this child would take people from all the nations of the earth.

It was at this time that the Lord imparted the name, House of David, into our hearts. From that day forward, the huge baby of my vision had a name, a calling, and a purpose. We had something to begin standing in faith to accomplish.

In my opinion, one of the primary keys to the success of House of David Ministries is that we have held true to the revelation that was given by the Holy Spirit. From its inception, House of David has been a house for all nations, a house for all people. It would not survive within a traditional church model, but it has thrived with access to the people from around the world.

Of course, this vison came before we had any knowledge of or experience with the live streaming capabilities the internet would offer. Through the technology that is available today, House of David is fulfilling that which the Holy Spirit imparted before the ministry existed outside of our hearts.

When God birthed House of David Ministries, which is now our congregation in Oklahoma, He did so at the home and farm of Tim, Sandy, and Brian Alsbaugh. At that time we believed that part of our collective foundational purpose was to further a movement.

In the previous chapter, we looked at what the apostle Paul called the "one new man"— Jews and Gentiles working successfully together with covenant power. This is what we see happening at House of David, and seeing it has finally brought me to a place of peace. We are finally established in our God-given identity and not striving to be anyone else.

We have, quite literally, returned to the Father's table. Founding House of David has taught us many things, but a few stand out:

- In every new venture, seek the Lord and wait on the Holy Spirit in prayer and meditation before allowing people (including yourself) to cloud the vision with carnal ideas. This is empowered vision.
- Stay true to the vision and revelation that God gives you. Do not take your square peg and force it into a round hole. This is empowered wisdom.
- Exponential success will be accomplished by managing and maintaining the true roots of the original vision. This is empowered success.
- When we desire to enter into a deeper relationship with our heavenly Father, His enabling flows in and through us to create a new perception and reality of who we are in the Messiah. This is empowered identity and purpose.

One of the important aspects of walking in empowerment with the Father is making His wisdom, knowledge, and understanding a priority in our lives. This means we need to carve out time to quiet our souls and to be alone with God. We need to find a quiet place to meditate and slow down as we read the Word or a favorite devotional. Listening to soft worship music ("soaking" music) can help prepare the atmosphere. But what matters most is waiting on the Lord. We must make space for *emunah*, because it demands being unhurried, confident of what God has promised, and resting enough to stand in the place where we are called to be a beacon for Yeshua.

Quieting our souls and waiting, however, is not the same thing as being passive. The opposite is true, in fact. It takes a great deal of discipline and desire to be able to successfully adopt and implement these changes in our own lives. Correction in our spiritual life can be as challenging as changes in our physical life, but a key in both areas is knowing that we can do all things through the Messiah who gives us strength (Philippians 4:13). We would be wise to never discount the supernatural power of the Holy Spirit. Calling on the Holy Spirit should be our first option for both the physical and spiritual challenges set before us.

I once attended an Israel Defense Force ceremony where the leadership gave each new recruit a Bible and a rifle. As the recruits held the Bible in one hand and the rifle in the other, they were told something along the lines of:

Today as you become a member of the Israel Defense Force, we give you a Bible and rifle and we pray that all you ever have to use is the Bible and remember that that which is etched into the great menorah of Israel [located outside the Knesset Parliament building in Jerusalem]:

"Not by might nor by power, but by My Spirit,"
Says the LORD of hosts. (Zechariah 4:6)

In your life there will be times where you have to use your rifle—so to speak—but it must be understood that the victory you will have with your "rifle" comes from the knowledge that you overcome with the Spirit, not human might.

After receiving a prophetic word from God, many people make the mistake that they simply wait and do nothing. They do not act but just wait for the door to open, the letter to arrive in the mail, or the phone to ring with the good news that the task has been accomplished. But God is proactive. God always does something. So waiting on God does not mean that we sit and do

nothing. When the Word tells us to "stand still and see the salvation of the LORD" (2 Chronicles 20:17), this is not instruction to
wait in a corner with our hands folded. It's a reminder to stand
our ground by faith.

In Hebrew, the word translated "stand still" in the New King
James Version is *yatsab*, which is used forty-eight times in the Old
Testament. It means to "station oneself"[7] and was used to describe
someone taking a stand in a battle or presenting himself at the
temple to stand before God.

In order to stand still in this way, we have to be prepared,
and part of the preparation is changing any behavior and attitudes
that are not consistent with God's Word. This is what enables us
to walk in faith and have victory in our assignments. This preparation period is a time when we are set free from all the doubt,
pride, and fear that can sabotage even the very best attempts at
completing an assignment in a new season.

The waiting period between proclamation and activation is
a time of preparing and repairing your life for your new battle
assignment.

That is *emunah*. That is *faith*.

fifteen

SHALOM

> The work of righteousness will be peace,
> And the effect of righteousness, quietness and
> assurance forever.
> My people will dwell in a peaceful habitation,
> In secure dwellings, and in quiet resting places.
> —ISAIAH 32:17–18

WHEN I RECONNECTED with my biological father, Joe, it was bizarre to learn how much like him I was. I had not been raised in his home, but our preferences were glaringly similar. We even enjoyed the same food and activities. Obviously, this was not a matter of culture. It was not learned, nurtured behavior or something I'd picked up by osmosis. It was DNA—or maybe even something deeper in my spirit.

I cannot express to you the peace and the joy that was birthed within my soul as a result of knowing why I was the way that I was. It was like a sigh of relief. It was contentment. It was *shalom*—"peace; completeness; welfare; health."[1]

Here's just one example. My adoptive father, Ray, suffered from motion sickness and got seasick easily. As a result he did not enjoy boating, fishing, or the ocean. I cannot say that I blame him, but I never understood it because from a very young age I loved everything about the ocean and water—boating, fishing, sailing, surfing, scuba diving, you name it.

My biological father, Joe, on the other hand, had actually made a living going out on the ocean as a fishing boat captain, and his father, my grandfather, had been both a sailor and a fisherman. My biological heritage was from two men of the sea. I was literally the son of a son of a sailor. It was obvious I had gotten my love of the water from my biological roots, even though I didn't discover those roots until I was well into my thirties.

Our souls—made up of mind, will, and emotions—will naturally gravitate toward a pattern of particular likes and dislikes because of what has been implanted in us from our past and even from our ancestors. Even our interests and tastes may come from a place that is deeply rooted in our DNA. For example, we've noticed that our two-year-old granddaughter, Ariebella, has some interesting food preferences.

It seems very strange that such a small child would like things like fresh Parmesan, blue cheese, and olives of all types—food that has such strong and pronounced flavors. However, those have been her favorites since she started eating solid foods, strong evidence that she inherited these distinctive preferences, just as I inherited some of mine. Ariebella has a tremendous advantage that I did not. She is being raised with her biological parents and grandparents who understand who she is and why she is the way she is.

As I mentioned before, my adoptive father, Ray, used to frequently comment, "I don't know where Curtis gets this." He always said this when I showed a taste for a "foreign" food or liked something no one else in the family did. It was a running joke in our family, but it didn't always feel funny to me, and the differences in our personal tastes sometimes made it difficult for us to relate to one another. So much was lost in translation, so to speak. It was never a big problem, just a subtle disconnect that reminded me that, biologically, I wasn't really a Landry.

I think a lot of us experience a similar thing in the spirit. We are all made "in the image of God" and meant to have stewardship and dominion over the earth (Genesis 1:26–28). This is meant to be done in relationship—in covenant partnership—with the Father. And He has built into each of us certain tastes, likes and dislikes, skills and abilities, and interests and passions that are more aligned with heaven than with our physical DNA. We are drawn to our proper identity, purpose, and destiny by what God planted within us before we were even born.

Not only that, but we are also predisposed to be people of justice, righteousness, and *shalom*, made to inherit a kingdom that is "righteousness and peace and joy in the Holy Spirit" (Romans 14:17). This is why certain aspects of the world upset our moral compasses, why broken relationships are so painful, and why abuse and violence are so traumatic and their effects so lasting, though God is able to heal us from them if we ask Him.

We are all just sojourners here, meant for a better world. But so often we fall for a false, counterfeit identity instead of this true one. We embrace idols instead of the one true God.

In my younger days, as I've already shared, I was a good businessman. I was a pretty good husband and father, and I guess I wasn't a bad man. But I wasn't great. My personal life was not exceptional. I certainly was not living in heart peace. Looking back, I now see that I spent the first thirty-six years of my life on a quest for things—not for truth—and my goal in life was happiness (*my* happiness) and not fulfillment. I had completely walked away from all things that had anything to do with God at that point. I'd rejected religion because my experiences of God as a child had been limited and off-putting.

At thirty-six, I had no idea of what it meant to really know God. Even after He interrupted my self-destructive ways and brought me to the Messiah, I still felt like I was only halfway home. It wasn't until I was also reconnected with my personal Jewish roots and, subsequently, the Jewish heritage of my Christian faith, that I was truly able to step into the fullness of knowing my heavenly Father and being the son He had called me to be.

It wasn't just a matter of knowing my physical and spiritual heritage either. That was merely the first step. There were still some things I needed to step into, ways I needed to change. I'm not talking about duties I had to fulfill and laws I needed to obey. What I'm talking about is aligning my ways with His ways so that I could operate under an open heaven—in direct relationship with my heavenly Father.

God wants to bless His children, but He is hindered in doing that when we insist on operating in our own ways rather than His. Blessings when we walk in falseness bring difficulties with them, and ultimately are no blessings at all. God, however, wants His blessings to remain complication free, so that we will "prosper in all things and be in health, just as [our] soul prospers" (3 John 2). That way we'll be able to live out the truth of Proverbs 10:22:

> The blessing of the LORD makes one rich,
> And He adds no sorrow with it.

The Hebrew word used to describe this state of blessing is *shalom. Vine's Complete Expository Dictionary of Old and New Testament Words* tells us:

Shalom is a very important term in the Old Testament and has maintained its place in Mishnaic, rabbinic, and modern Hebrew. In Israel today, people greet the newcomer and each other with the words *mah shlomka*, ("what is your peace," "how are you doing,") and they ask about the "peace" ("well-being") of one's family. . . . *Shalom* as a harmonious state of the soul and mind encourages the development of the faculties and powers. The state of being at ease is experienced both externally and internally. In Hebrew it finds expression in the phrase *beshalom* ("in peace"): *"I will both lay me down in peace [beshalom], and sleep: for thou, Lord, only makest me dwell in safety"* (Psalm 4:8).[2]

I learned early in my walk with the Lord that how I invested my time determined how I prospered with God. As I reconnected with my Jewish roots, I discovered that not only did observing the Jewish holidays put me into rhythm with heaven but so did observing the Sabbath—not "the Sabbath" as many think of Sunday today, but *Shabbat*, the Jewish Sabbath that begins at sundown on Friday night and ends at sundown on Saturday. We attend services at House of David on Friday nights, where a meal is shared before a celebration service. We light candles, welcome the Sabbath with the Sabbath blessing, blow shofars, worship, teach, pray, and make an offering. We try our best to rest together as a family on Saturday and honor the Lord.

But observing Sabbath is about more than the day of the week. Setting aside a weekly Sabbath rest allows me time to seek the Lord, refresh my soul, and refocus on life's priorities. It creates a break between the events of last week and of next week and gives me space to prioritize time with God. It means sanctifying my time by disciplining myself to rest on the Sabbath and meditate on the Lord—in much the same way that my wife and I sanctify our finances with tithes and offerings. We set them aside as sacred, apart from the everyday and ordinary.

I am not legalistic about the Sabbath, but I have found great peace in setting aside time to rest, time with my family, and some one-on-one time with God. It is a day when I step back from the world and focus on gratitude for God's many blessings in my life.

Two of God's mysteries that Christie and I have found to be success keys are:

- In consistency lies the victory.
- Moderation in all things breeds steady progress.

We try to apply both keys as we surrender to God in the area of time management and explore the blessings that come with keeping the Sabbath. We try to follow Yeshua's principle that "the Sabbath was made for man, not man for the Sabbath" (Mark 2:27). And yet we want to follow the intention of God's instructions in Exodus as closely as possible:

> Remember the Sabbath day, to keep it holy. Six days you shall labor and do all your work, but the seventh day is the Sabbath of the LORD your God. In it you shall do no work: you, nor your son, nor your daughter, nor your male servant, nor your female servant, nor your cattle, nor your stranger who is within your gates. For in six days the LORD made the heavens and the earth, the sea, and all that is in them, and rested the seventh day. Therefore the LORD blessed the Sabbath day and hallowed it. (Exodus 20:8–11)

But what exactly does it mean to keep a day holy?

The word *holy* in Hebrew is *kadosh*. *Hakadosh* refers to the "Holy One" who is "utterly unique, distinct, sacred, and set

apart."[3] As we dig into the book of Genesis, we can see that after
God spent six days creating the world and all that is in it, including men and women, He rested on the seventh day. By doing so,
He gave us the first principles of time management right there in
Genesis 1. Not only did He cause the sun to rise and set on a daily
basis, delineating time for work and rest, but He also set aside an
entire day for a Sabbath rest. Keeping the Sabbath holy means that
we set aside an entire day as well, doing what we can to make the
day unique, distinct, sacred, and set apart.

Understanding the feasts of the Lord, the Sabbath rest,
tithes and offerings, and all traditions that are rooted in the Old
Testament has been a major part of my own personal quest for
truth. And I know many others who have found that reconnecting with our roots, our inheritance, and our promises in God on a
weekly basis empowers us in our purpose.

Every week we are bombarded with false narratives and dis-
couragements, but when we observe a Sabbath and set aside time
with the Holy One, we are reestablished in the truth in our souls
so that we can stay on track. We must take time to shut out the
voices of the world and listen to the voice of God on a weekly basis
at least. This may well mean taking a retreat from social media
and even the news.

Here's an analogy I find helpful. Our minds are sensory-based
gardens, our eyes and ears are our primary means of seeding
our gardens, and what we allow to be planted determines what
will eventually grow. When we let unhealthy seeds be planted, we
shouldn't be surprised when unhealthy things grow. As Yeshua said:

> A good man out of the good treasure of his heart brings forth
> good; and an evil man out of the evil treasure of his heart
> brings forth evil. For out of the abundance of the heart his
> mouth speaks. (Luke 6:45)

Now, obviously, we can't keep out all the wayward seeds that may land in our gardens. But we can pluck out the weeds on a regular basis and be intentional about cultivating plants that will yield good fruit. I have found that being intentional about what I see and hear and do on this set-apart day helps me to do this. But even more important, it helps me align myself to God's way of doing things and His view of time.

Time is a treasure to the Lord as long as we are listening to Him, and I have learned the hard way that trying to pry open doors that God wants shut is a waste of time. We can't plow our way into our destiny through humanly engineered thoughts and practices. God's plans need to be implemented God's way. He's not in a hurry, and He doesn't push His "employees" to the breaking point. God does not operate outside of peace—*shalom*—so why would we ever expect that we should do that in serving Him? In fact, He's even at peace when everything else is in chaos. As the storm raged and the disciples panicked, Yeshua slept (Mark 4:37–40).

God's peace and strength always align with God's timing and will. No matter how difficult the task, if we do it in God's timing and according to His instructions, the impossible becomes possible through His supernatural power. Personal striving and manipulation only hinder God's favor, while faith and patience increase it.

Which would you rather walk in?

When God is in control, He wants to sit in the driver's seat, and we have to trust Him with our destination and our time of arrival. Sometimes we labor for what we think we want, only to discover that it is not what we need at all. Life is a series of trials, tests, and discoveries. If we have a teachable spirit, all tests and trials will become profitable for building our character.

A man of God once spoke a word of wisdom to Christie and me. He said, "Go where you are celebrated, not tolerated." This has turned out to be a great point of truth in our lives and a key to living more and more into God's *shalom*. Often we humans desire to be celebrated for advancement and promotion in areas that do not agree with God's plans for our lives, and therefore we struggle and sometimes fail in our attempt to gain soulish approval. When you go where you are celebrated and not tolerated, it is a place where the atmosphere and people are celebrating the gift of God in you and desire to see it shared. It may not be an easy venue but it is not hostile against you and your gift. Through the years, I have learned that God is not into shortcuts. He wants us to learn and absorb wisdom from every minute of every day. He's always trying to teach us something for our betterment.

Whether you are Jewish or Gentile, observing a Sabbath's rest can be a powerful way to align yourself with what God wants to do in your life. It's a designated time to turn off the mental computer that endlessly whirs and churns and to reboot it with the truth of God's Word. It may be time for you to refresh the OS of your divine Creator—the Author and Finisher of your faith.

There's nothing wrong with taking a physical rest as part of a Sabbath observance, but I find that spending part of the day immersed in Scripture can be enormously refreshing as well as spiritually edifying. God's Word is unique compared to any other words you will read because they are spirit and they are life. God's Word is healing and energizing and encouraging to our souls, and spending in-depth time with it on a weekly basis will not only reenergize you but also redirect you to the vision and purpose that God has given you. I can guarantee you that when you set aside time to rest in God's Word, you will actually get more done—not less. Doing this is not wasting time. It is redeeming time.

It is redeeming life.

It is redeeming you.

Your next exponential creative idea is not going to come from the inspiration of your overloaded carnal mind, but from the regenerated spiritual mind that is tapped into its biblical roots. If you are going to be in the right mental space for that to happen, you must set aside time for it. You can live a good life with God, or you can live your best life with God. How deeply you understand your roots—and how consistently you set aside time to be with your heavenly Father—determines good, better, or best.

If you can imagine with me for a moment, picture a father walking hand in hand with a child. All the father's love and experience is always available to the young and inexperienced child, but the child is not always in a place to receive it. The child does not need to know or understand what the daddy knows to be protected and provided for. All he or she needs to do is remain connected—hand in hand—with the father. That way, what is needed will always be available when it is needed and when the child grows up enough to be ready for it.

I remember walking with my Ariebella on the beautifully green and manicured golf course near our house. She was about a year and a half at the time, and the only words I could understand from her were *Saba*—which is what she calls me—and *go*. Everything else was a guess. But as I walked with her that day, I had a Father God experience. We walked in "green pastures" and were led beside the "still waters" of beautiful ponds (Psalm 23:2), and our time together definitely restored my soul (v. 3).

I don't know why, but it reminded me of a time when my father, Ray, was holding my hand leading me into the ocean waves. Some of my earliest memories are of how big those California coastal waves were and how safe I felt as long as I held onto his hand. As I remembered, I was thinking about how excited Ariebella was to be walking on this beautifully green fairway with space to run and be free—while safely in my care.

Our Father in heaven longs for times like that with each of us.

And when we let ourselves slow down and hold His hand, something remarkable happens. Our vision expands and our space enlarges so that we can experience freedom, awe, peace (*shalom*), love, and safety. Such times of resting in Him will be some of the greatest you will experience this side of heaven.

The Jewish roots of our faith clearly teach and remind us that we have been grafted into this tree that is holy—our God of Abraham, Isaac, and Jacob. The more we understand and experience our godly inheritance in the Bible through our Jewish roots, the more we can enjoy our sojourn on the earth, despite being in "enemy territory." For in the sap of His glory that travels from the roots is the power of the Holy Spirit that carries identity, purpose, and destiny so that we can leave a legacy to our children's children—a legacy of the hope and glory of being in covenant with God, whose promises are always *yes* and *amen*.

> For the Son of God, Jesus Christ, who was preached among you by us—by me, Silvanus, and Timothy—was not Yes and No, but in Him was Yes. For all the promises of God in Him are Yes, and in Him Amen, to the glory of God through us. Now He who establishes us with you in Christ and has anointed us is God, who also has sealed us and given us the Spirit in our hearts as a guarantee. (2 Corinthians 1:19–22)

The word *truth* in Hebrew is *emeth*, which also carries connotations of reliability, sureness, stability, and faithfulness.[4] At some level, we are all on a quest for that. We are all seeking stability in our purpose. We are all seeking the faithfulness of God.

In the Bible we find that the first place this word is used is Genesis 24:48 when Abraham's servant said: "And I bowed my head and worshiped the LORD, and blessed the LORD God of my master Abraham, *who had led me in the way of truth*."

God guided Abraham's servant in the right way. The sure way. God was faithful to him and God will be faithful to you as you continue on your own quest for truth.

May you and your family live in the rich heritage of your faith.

May you and your family live in *emeth*.

And especially, may you and your family live always in the *shalom* of Yeshua.

sixteen

MULTIPLICATION

*Now may He who supplies seed to the sower, and
bread for food, supply and multiply the seed you have
sown and increase the fruits of your righteousness,
while you are enriched in everything for all liberality,
which causes thanksgiving through us to God. For
the administration of this service not only supplies
the needs of the saints, but also is abounding through
many thanksgivings to God, while, through the proof
of this ministry, they glorify God for the obedience of
your confession to the gospel of Christ, and for your
liberal sharing with them and all men.*

—2 CORINTHIANS 9:10–13

ONE OF THE MOST POWERFUL benefits of living in
covenant and being empowered by the Father is the gift of
multiplication—the ability to expand our blessings and create

abundance. When we are living in alignment with covenant, multiplication is a given. It's a promise right of the blessings of the Abrahamic and Mosaic covenants:

> The LORD will open to you his good treasury, the heavens, to give the rain to your land in its season and to bless all the work of your hands. And you shall lend to many nations, but you shall not borrow. And the LORD will make you the head and not the tail, and you shall only go up and not down, if you obey the commandments of the LORD your God, which I command you today, being careful to do them. (Deuteronomy 28:12–13 ESV)

According to *Strong's Exhaustive Concordance*, the Hebrew word for "multiply" is *rabah*, which is a verb meaning "to increase (in whatever respect)—(bring in) abundance . . . be in authority . . . enlarge, excel . . . be full of . . . heap, increase . . . multiply, nourish, plenty(-eous) . . . store."[1] This word first appears in Genesis 1:28:

> Then God blessed them, and God said to them, "Be fruitful and *multiply*; fill the earth and subdue it; have dominion over the fish of the sea, over the birds of the air, and over every living thing that moves on the earth." (emphasis added)

Note that multiplication is not only a gift but a command: we are *commanded* to be fruitful and multiply. It was actually the very first instruction—and the first blessing—that God gave to creation (Genesis 1:22) and then to humanity (Genesis 1:28). We were instructed to fill the earth, subdue it, and take dominion. And this was not just about procreation, but a lifestyle of stewardship toward all that God entrusted us with, a responsibility to take whatever blessings we have and be intentional about increasing them.

The Jewish mind-set understands abundance as part of the blessings of their covenant with God. Jews expect it to happen and have no qualms about accepting it and building on it. As I mentioned in the first chapter, there are really no vows of poverty in Judaism. To have nothing is to have nothing to give, and to not give is to deny the nature of the Father. It is considered a matter of faithfulness to have more than enough so that there is a surplus with which we can be generous, and a matter of wisdom to set aside resources for future need. When the Old Testament speaks of having more than enough, it's because that's what following its guidance will bring us. This biblical mentality is completely countercultural to the "spend to your last penny, then put the rest on your credit card" mentality of most Americans today.

To Jews, having a generous spirit means to give graciously out of abundance, not out of lack. Their example is Abraham tithing to Melchizedek, not the widow giving her last two mites. And many Christians who have rediscovered their Jewish roots can testify that adopting this attitude toward both material and spiritual blessings can be powerfully transformative.

Sacrificial giving does have its place, of course, as we'll discuss later in terms of the boy who gave his lunch to feed the multitude. But I am convinced that God never intended sacrifice to be the norm that the church has made it today. God doesn't think in terms of limitations or have a spirit of poverty. How could He? And we are to think like Him.

The third person of the Trinity, the Holy Spirit, only operates through generosity, not out of lack. The Holy Spirit does not communicate to us in terms of lack. The Holy Spirit does not dream in lack. It's impossible for the Holy Spirit to engage with us in anything but generosity. If He asks us to give sacrificially, it's because He knows of the abundance obedience brings.

There's no financial pressure in heaven. In order to hear God and to understand Him, we have to be able to speak the same language of abundance that is the language of an open heaven.

Observant Jews are reminded of this as part of the *havdalah* service that takes place at the end of the Sabbath and the beginning of the new week. In his book, *Thou Shalt Prosper*, Rabbi Daniel Lapin shares that *havdalah* is a ceremony of song and ritual. A prayer is recited over a cup, into which wine is poured until it overflows into the saucer the cup is sitting on. The prayer is one that asks for multiplication of offspring and wealth so that the family may always have more than enough.

Havdalah also commemorates what work is all about, which is why it is observed at the start of the workweek, not the end. It is a reminder that human beings have six days in which to prosper. As Rabbi Lapin pointed out, the *havdalah* prayer highlights the hands and by extension whatever work those hands do. It asks for prosperity in whatever work those hands undertake. Letting the wine overflow symbolizes the need to work hard enough to have a surplus, not just barely enough to get by. Rabbi Lapin wrote,

> This overflowing cup symbolizes the intention to produce during the workweek ahead not only sufficient to fill one's cup, but also an excess that will allow overflow for the benefit of others. In other words, I am obliged to first fill my cup and then continue pouring as it were, so that I will have sufficient to give away to others, thus helping to jump-start their own efforts. Judaism views attending to your own vineyard not as shameful, but as a moral obligation.[2]

This is part of what God means when He commands us in Genesis 1:28 to increase and take dominion (*memshalah*—"rule," "realm," "government, power"[3]). This idea is a complete antithesis to the spirit of poverty, vows of poverty, and doctrines of lack.

We need to be aware, however, that the principle of multiplication works for both good and evil. Whatever is multiplied will increase "according to its kind." We can see this principle at work from the very beginning:

> Then God said, "Let the earth bring forth the living creature according to its kind: cattle and creeping thing and beast of the earth, each according to its kind"; and it was so. And God made the beast of the earth according to its kind, cattle according to its kind, and everything that creeps on the earth according to its kind. And God saw that it was good. (Genesis 1:24–25)

"According to its kind" is stated five times in these two verses, punctuating the principle that we multiply according to our kind—*good* or *bad*.

This principle goes hand in hand with one of the basic laws God built into the universe: seedtime and harvest.

> While the earth remains,
> Seedtime and harvest,
> Cold and heat,
> Winter and summer,
> And day and night
> Shall not cease.
>
> (Genesis 8:22)

The combination of these two principles gives us tremendous power to control our destiny. By sowing seeds into our lives, we can create abundance in our lives.

What are the seeds in your life? They can be words, work, time, activities, or money. It can be resources and knowledge. But again, the principles of seedtime and harvest and of multiplication can apply to almost anything in our lives—positive or negative. Which is why, again, we need to be careful—especially concerning what we allow into our minds, which is where everything starts.

You probably remember a childhood song that warns us to be careful what our eyes see, what our ears hear, and what our mouths say. What is the purpose of such warnings? Because our eyes, ears, and mouths are gateways into our minds, we're wise to be cautious about what sights, sounds, ideas, or other input we let in through our eyes and ears, and what we come into agreement with or seed with our mouths. We sow and reap according to these things.

The Bible addresses this reality in the first psalm:

> Blessed is the man
> Who walks not in the counsel of the ungodly,
> Nor stands in the path of sinners,
> Nor sits in the seat of the scornful;
> But his delight is in the law of the LORD,
> And in His law he meditates day and night.
> He shall be like a tree
> Planted by the rivers of water,
> That brings forth its fruit in its season,
> Whose leaf also shall not wither;
> And whatever he does shall prosper.
>
> (PSALM 1:1–3)

Note the emphasis here on who we spend time with. This is important because who we associate with and seek counsel from affects the way we think. There is a principle among the up and coming that "Your income will be the average of the five people you spend the most time with." Why? Not because they will pay you, but because they will elevate your thinking.

Multiplication begins in our thought lives; the mind is the seat of both poverty and prosperity. Third John 2 speaks to this reality: "Beloved, I pray that you may prosper in all things and be in health, just as your soul [made up of mind, will, and emotions] prospers." If you want to be a person who has a generous spirit and has more than enough to give, and if you want to get in on the big things God wants to do on the earth today, you must pay attention to the thoughts and assumptions you have allowed to flourish inside your head. In particular, you must clear your mind of any association of poverty with holiness and any lingering assumptions that wealth in itself is evil.

Money is a neutral thing, a medium of exchange, and just a tool that can be used to create something else. Having it or not having it doesn't say anything about the character of your heart, which is where true holiness is seated. Money can reveal what is in your heart—as we see with the greedy or with those who villainize the rich—but it doesn't cause it. A healthy heart comes through relationship with the Father, not a lack of material blessings.

Think about it: If money and wealth were inherently evil, why would God have given so much instruction on how to live in safety and in prosperity during our time on the earth? The Bible talks about money more than any other topic except salvation. And for what it's worth, the Bible does not say that "money is the root of all evil," as some of us have been taught. The Bible says, "The *love of money* is a root of all kinds of evil, for which some have strayed from the faith in their greediness" (1 Timothy 6:10). That verse is talking about greed, not wealth.

We can have better lives and a better world if we will return to our biblical roots and live by biblical principles. One of my personal major motivations for writing this book is that it can be a gift to share and imparts a revelation of the things I have learned. These are lessons that have greatly impacted both Christie and me, as well as our family and our ministries. They are principles that work—spiritual keys that change lives.

The Old Testament lays out several important keys for multiplication. One is that multiplication isn't something that simply happens to us. Our full participation is required. Personally, I have always had great difficulty with the belief or thought that "whatever happens, happens." My family and our ministry haven't gotten to where we are today—able to participate in the giving of tens of millions of dollars worth of aid to support Israel and the other causes we care about—by thinking we'd just let whatever happens happen. The choices we make and the intentions we put into play matter; good choices yield good results. And what we teach to others—especially our children—matters too. We multiply our blessings when we teach others so that they can successfully walk in God's laws of multiplication as well.

Another vital Old Testament principle of multiplication is one of the most important: when we give, we multiply. Let that thought and mind-set sink in. When we give away, we multiply. We do not decrease. We increase.

This principle is intrinsic to the Old Testament practice of leaving part of a harvest for gleaners, as spelled out by Moses in Leviticus 19 and Deuteronomy 24:

> When you reap the harvest of your land, you shall not reap your field right up to its edge, neither shall you gather the gleanings after your harvest. And you shall not strip your vineyard bare, neither shall you gather the fallen grapes of your vineyard. You shall leave them for the poor and for the sojourner: I am the LORD your God. (Leviticus 19:9–10 ESV)

> When you reap your harvest in your field and forget a sheaf in the field, you shall not go back to get it. It shall be for the

sojourner, the fatherless, and the widow, that the LORD your
God may bless you in all the work of your hands. When you
beat your olive trees, you shall not go over them again. It shall
be for the sojourner, the fatherless, and the widow. When
you gather the grapes of your vineyard, you shall not strip it
afterward. It shall be for the sojourner, the fatherless, and the
widow. You shall remember that you were a slave in the land
of Egypt; therefore I command you to do this. (Deuteronomy
24:19–22 ESV)

This system was designed as a way for the poor to survive
without having their dignity taken from them, as is often done
today with government or nonprofit aid. It gave the poor the
opportunity to work and provide for themselves. It also helped
the givers remember that all their blessings came from God in
the first place and that these blessings were to be multiplied and
shared.

Many believers struggle reading through Leviticus and even
Deuteronomy because they feel that these books are not relatable.
("We're no longer under the old law anymore, right?") But the
principle of gleaning and the richness of the covenant blessing
behind it may in fact be more important today than ever. When
we let others glean from the field of our lives, we will never do
without. We will not live in lack. We will not suffer with unmet
needs.

How does this translate into the way we live today? It means
being generous in business and employment. It means not taking
every bit of what is rightfully ours, but instead finding ways for
some of it to support and employ those who are among the poor,
the aliens, the foreigners, or the strangers.

When we live like this, we are following the Father's example
and His nature of giving abundantly and graciously. We are

confirming in our lives that the biblical principles of giving and multiplication still hold. We are adhering to a Matthew 6:33 life-style of seeking first the kingdom of God and His justice and fairness—*tzedakah*, as talked about at the beginning of chapter 11. And we are living in obedience to Yeshua's instruction that we follow the two greatest commandments in all Scripture:

> "You shall love the LORD your God with all your heart, with all your soul, with all your mind, and with all your strength." This is the first commandment. And the second, like it, is this: "You shall love your neighbor as yourself." There is no other commandment greater than these. (Mark 12:30–31)

By the way, if you want to see a beautiful example of glean-ing and how it can redeem, read the book of Ruth, which we also touched on briefly in chapter 1. I'm sorry that we don't have more space for it here, because the story of Ruth and Boaz is an incredible testimony that teaches us about the power of giving to multiply in every area of our lives. It also tells the family back-ground of King David, from whose line the Messiah, Yeshua the Redeemer, would come (Luke 3:23–37).

Multiplication is a kingdom principle that also makes room for us to leave a legacy to others—and legacy is more than money. Yeshua said it best when He instructed us to "lay up" our trea-sures in heaven, not on earth (Matthew 6:19). Our focus must be on our assignment and not on accumulating wealth just to fill up bigger storehouses. Remember the parable Yeshua told:

> The ground of a certain rich man yielded plentifully. And he thought within himself, saying, "What shall I do, since I have no room to store my crops?" So he said, "I will do this: I will pull down my barns and build greater, and there I will

store all my crops and my goods. And I will say to my soul, 'Soul, you have many goods laid up for many years; take your ease; eat, drink, and be merry.'" But God said to him, "Fool! This night your soul will be required of you; then whose will those things be which you have provided?" So is he who lays up treasure for himself, and is not rich toward God. (Luke 12:16–21)

As we mentioned in chapter 11, Yeshua wasn't critical of the man having barns. Everyone listening to Him that day had barns at home and at least a year's surplus of seed in their storehouses. The problem was that this man's surplus had no purpose outside his own greed and gluttony.

This is where stewardship comes in. The Bible balances a positive view of abundance with an emphasis on responsibility. We have the ability to multiply blessings, but we also have a responsibility to use those blessings wisely and according to God's covenant principles.

It can be a difficult and soul-challenging discipline to balance budgets and spiritual responsibilities within our lives. But that's the point. The challenge should be constantly driving us back to our knees in front of the Father, because, as we saw in chapter 9, "for everyone to whom much is given, from him much will be required; and to whom much has been committed, of him they will ask the more" (Luke 12:48).

One of the greatest challenges I have personally faced as a founder and leader of organizations is balancing the practical with the spiritual. This is a challenge we will all face at some point in our journeys, because living by faith could almost be translated as "living by risking that God will deliver what He says." I have trained myself over the years to understand that the bigger the responsibility ahead of me, the bigger my faith in God must be.

In order to have a testimony, in other words, we must first have a test.

This is particularly true in the area of finances. Our ministries have always initially lacked resources when trying to tackle a God assignment, and this lack has required us to step out in faith again and again, walking "by faith, not by sight" (2 Corinthians 5:7). Kingdom assignments are only conquered in kingdom ways.

When you are in a financial bind, when things are tight and bills are piling up, instead of following your carnal mind and focusing on what you do not have, you must allow your spirit to take over and focus on what you *do* have, because God can only multiply what you have, not what you don't. That's just how multiplication works. A bazillion times nothing is still nothing, but even very small amounts, when offered in faith, can yield big results. Giving is always the answer for lack.

Most of us are familiar with the story of the feeding of the five thousand. Some translations label it as "the miracle of the five loaves and the two fishes." The key principle in this story is that even the tiny amount the young boy had was enough when it was totally surrendered to Yeshua.

Five loaves and two fishes were not nearly enough for a multitude, but fully surrendered to God, it was more than enough. Once the boy's gift was given, it not only fed a crowd of five thousand men (plus women and children), but twelve baskets of fragments were left over after all had eaten and were full.

Something interesting to note: five loaves plus two fish equals seven elements. In biblical numerology, seven represents the number of perfection. Twelve, the number of baskets filled with leftovers, is the number of government (the idea of dominion, remember, is connected to government). When we sow in perfection, in obedience to God's Word, we reap dominion—favor and multiplication.

> A man's gift makes room for him,
> And brings him before great men.
>
> (PROVERBS 18:16)

Once again, this doesn't just apply to money. When the widow at Zarephath faced starvation for herself and her son, God multiplied the flour in her bin when she shared it with the prophet (1 Kings 17:8–16). When another widow needed to pay the collectors threatening to take her sons as slaves, God multiplied her oil according to the number of vessels she set out (2 Kings 4:1–7).

What do you have and what do you need? When you place both before the Lord, the principle of multiplication kicks in and changes the whole picture. But you have to give before you can receive. If you need wisdom, sow what you know. If you need favor, show favor to others. If you need good connections, be a connector.

These are all things that you should be doing anyway because success demands all these things. Plus, being generous with this is another way to exercise your generous heart. Networking and favor need to multiply along with your resources.

One of the keys to attracting the right people into your network is being a giver. Good people are attracted to generous and charitable hearts. And it is reassuring to know that we cannot out-give God.

The Old Testament concept of mercy fits beautifully here. Most Christian theologians will define *mercy* as something like "compassion or forgiveness, even when undeserved." However, the Hebrew word for mercy is *chesed*, and it envelops so much more than compassion and forgiveness. That word represents the attitude that drives us to constantly be thinking of ways to bless our covenant partner. It is the word used to describe the loving-kindness or steadfast love of God. *Chesed* is faithfulness. *Chesed* is covenant.

A man in Israel spoke into my life very early on when he said "*Chesed* was a seed sown and a seed received," meaning that if we need mercy, we should sow mercy. If we need something else, we should sow that. He went on to say, "You are a big *mattan*." *Mattan* is a name that is derived from the word *gift* and quite literally means "giving." In his somewhat broken English, he was trying to convey that my organization had brought gifts of mercy, *chesed*, to him and those in his region. It was one of the most generous compliments I've ever received.

It should be clear by this point that the key to multiplication is giving. When we plant good seeds, when we give out of our abundance, when we reach out to others in love and mercy, we increase our store of good things in kind. But there is another dimension to this principle, one that Yeshua taught in places like Luke 14:14: "You will be blessed, because they cannot repay you; for you shall be repaid at the resurrection of the just."

In other words, to use our lives to multiply in the lives of others, we often have to give the opposite of what has been given to us.

This concept can seem counterintuitive and even contradictory, and it's certainly not easy to live out, but it has powerful repercussions. Do you want to store up treasure in heaven? Give to those who cannot give back to you. If someone reacts to you in a hateful manner, you respond in love. If someone interacts with you in a depressed way, you respond in joy. If someone responds to you in a disruptive way, you respond in peace. If someone is continually an irritation, you respond in long-suffering. If someone is cruel, you respond in kindness. If someone is evil toward you, you respond in goodness. If someone lies or cheats, you respond in faithfulness and truth. If someone is short-tempered, you respond in gentleness and patience. And with those who are acting ridiculous toward you, you respond in self-control.

Against such responses—against love—there are no restrictions. No one has a legitimate, legal leg to stand on in opposing someone who loves like God loves. Your response of the opposite will multiply goodness and favor in every area of your life.

This level of spiritual discipline is the equivalent to having a black belt in love. It's like aikido, the martial art whose practitioners aim to protect their opponents even while defending themselves. The harder the other person attacks you, the more they hurt themselves.

The Holy Spirit can move with the angels of God at maximum force when we battle in the opposite spirit of the evil intended against us. This is a learned skill; I would call it spiritual character and maturity. But regardless of what you call it, it is an excellent way to multiply your influence and your testimony for Yeshua. I have watched these principles disarm even the most demonically oppressed people and can testify that it is true: love never fails.

When the young boy gave his lunch, Yeshua took the bread, lifted it up to the heavens, blessed it (*kadosh*—He separated it and made it holy), and broke it. He gave it to His disciples, they gave it to others, and the gift multiplied. In the same way, when you choose to live the lifestyle of a spiritual black belt—responding in the opposite spirit when evil attacks—every day you will lift up your life, bless it, set it apart as holy unto the Lord, break it, and give it away.

When we follow this principle of responding in the opposite spirit, we give up our right to be angry, to be offended, or to retaliate against those who would harm us. We follow Yeshua's counsel to turn the other cheek when struck or to give up our coat when asked for our tunic (Matthew 5:40). We forgive and forgive (Matthew 18:21–22). And as we do, we align ourselves with spiritual forces that produce favor and multiplication.

Ecclesiastes 11:1 suggests that nothing in our lives is truly lost:

> Cast your bread upon the waters,
> For you will find it after many days.

This proves true with so many areas of our lives. Cast your kindness upon the waters. Be a cheerful giver, and what you give will eventually come back to you—multiplied.

What we must always remember is that God is the original Giver. All good things in the world and in our lives come from Him, and it is He who takes our offerings and multiplies them into abundant blessings. The more we give into His kingdom mandate to be fruitful and multiply, the more we give generously out of our abundance, the more we help those who cannot help us, the more we give back good for evil, and the more we align ourselves with what He is doing in our world, the greater the return—both material and spiritual—we will experience in our lives. Yeshua Himself summed it up this way:

> Give, and it will be given to you: good measure, pressed down,
> shaken together, and running over will be put into your bosom.
> For with the same measure that you use, it will be measured
> back to you. (Luke 6:38)

seventeen

LEAVING A LEGACY
THAT EMPOWERS

But the steadfast love of the LORD is from everlasting
to everlasting on those who fear him,
and his righteousness to children's children,
to those who keep his covenant
and remember to do his commandments.

—PSALM 103:17–18 ESV

ONE OF OUR GROWING ORGANIZATIONS, My Olive
Tree, was birthed out of a heart to support the land and the people
of Israel. It is a project focused on legacy—on blessing many
generations to come.

In 2004 I sat with Israel's then finance minister, now Prime
Minister Benjamin Netanyahu, and we discussed a huge humani-
tarian initiative I was involved in—a project that would bring in
more than twenty million dollars' worth of aid to Israel. It was a

huge endeavor. The finance minister was polite and seemed grateful but also expressed a heartfelt concern: he did not want Israel to become dependent on charity from the outside. He desired to see the country prosper and have an economy that supported itself.

A few years later, the concept of My Olive Tree was presented to us by a group of Israelis from a kibbutz in the Galilee region. They wanted My Olive Tree to partner with them to plant one million olive trees all over their country, especially in desert regions.

At first I was overwhelmed and hesitant about their presentation. I liked the idea, but I felt sure that the undertaking was beyond our abilities. Then, however, I felt the prompting of the Holy Spirit, urging me to step outside our meeting place. When I responded, the Spirit showed me a vision of a blue and green globe like that which you would see in a photograph of the earth from space. As I gazed at it, the Lord spoke to me: *"You see all those little green spots? I planted all those without your help."* Then I remembered something David Ben-Gurion, the first prime minister of Israel, had once said: "If an expert says it can't be done, get another expert."

After that, my hesitation was gone. I wasn't up for God finding someone else to do this job. I was in. That is how My Olive Tree got started. Since that day this organization has partnered with sponsors around the world to plant nearly forty thousand olive trees in Israel. Yes, that's a far cry from our huge vision for one million, but we're not finished yet.[1]

It's not unusual for prophetic covenant promises to involve huge visions that will take generations to fulfill. In Genesis 22 we read that as Abraham was taking his covenant son, Isaac, to the place of sacrifice, he looked and "saw the place afar off" (v. 4). Then Abraham said, "We will come back" (v. 5).

I personally believe that when Abraham lifted his eyes, he saw a prophetic vision of the future and knew that all would be well, that he could trust God to take care of His covenant promise.

In fact, some believe that the place he saw from "afar off" was Golgotha, the hill on which Yeshua would be crucified—the place of redemption.

When it comes to My Olive Tree, I can see "afar off" too. I know that even if I do not get to see the one-millionth tree planted, our little Ariebella will. I see it as part of the heritage I leave for her to walk out.

When My Olive Tree first started sponsoring plantings, we focused on the Galilee area. It was extremely exciting to see our vision unfold as it literally took root in the Holy Land! A few years later, the doors opened for us to start planting in the desert. Like David Ben-Gurion, we had our hearts set on working in the Negev, so this opportunity breathed new life into the project for us as a family and for us as an organization.

It is incredible to know that our supporters are helping fulfill the words of the prophets by bringing the wastelands to life by expanding a greenbelt into the desert to create livable habitats for families to return to the land of their Father. More than anything, our sponsorships give hope and speak of friendship and solidarity. Our trees say to Israel and her people: "I see you. I believe in your history, your present, your future, and your right to exist. And as a fellow child of Abraham, I am standing with you and believing for the full manifestation of your covenant promises."

For us, planting an olive tree in Israel is not only a prophetic covenant act based on a vision of Israel's future but also an act of remembrance—honoring our roots and reclaiming the land. It is a prophetic act of standing with Israel and claiming the manifestation of her covenant promises while believing for our own.

> If I forget you, O Jerusalem,
> Let my right hand forget its skill!
> If I do not remember you,

Let my tongue cling to the roof of my mouth—
If I do not exalt Jerusalem
Above my chief joy.

(PSALM 137:5–6)

The city of Jerusalem is without a doubt the most significant city in the entire world, because it is the city where God put His name (2 Chronicles 6:6). It seems that the whole world battles to bless or curse the city of Jerusalem. Scripture says that we are not to forget her, in part because she is key to our future. A general concession among scholars and students of prophecy is that Jerusalem is God's end-time clock for mankind. Her fulfillment of Bible prophecy is an indicator of birth pangs for the return of Messiah, not only for Christians who await the second coming but also for the Jewish people who are still awaiting the "first coming," so to speak. Many scholars believe and understand that "as goes Jerusalem, so goes the world." She is a prophetic signpost.

My Olive Tree's footprint was further expanded in 2016 when the Israel Nature and Parks Authority approached us with a vision involving more than just olive trees. They asked us to plant the seven types of plants and produce mentioned in Deuteronomy 8:7–8, in a part of Jerusalem called the King's Valley:

> For the LORD your God is bringing you into a good land, a land of brooks of water, of fountains and springs, that flow out of valleys and hills; a land of wheat and barley, of vines and fig trees and pomegranates, a land of olive oil and honey.

The King's Valley, which is part of the larger Kidron Valley, is believed to have once been a garden for the ancient kings of Israel. It is located just east of the site of King David's palace. And perhaps most important, this area is located just below the Mount of Olives, where the Messiah is expected to return. It is an area where the kings of Israel once walked and where the Messiah of Israel will walk again. And just like a bride, the land is being prepared for the Bridegroom. As the prophet foresaw:

> In that day His feet will stand on the Mount of Olives
> Which faces Jerusalem on the east.
>
> (ZECHARIAH 14:4)

Our ministry is involved with preparing for that most historic day!

This unique project is more than just a land initiative or an ecological endeavor. It is also a fulfillment of a prayer. In Psalm 122:6–9, we are commanded to pray for the peace of Jerusalem.

> Pray for the peace of Jerusalem:
> "May they prosper who love you.
> Peace be within your walls,
> Prosperity within your palaces."
> For the sake of my brethren and companions,
> I will now say, "Peace be within you."
> Because of the house of the LORD our God
> I will seek your good.

The King's Valley is in a highly valuable and disputed area. Planting a peaceful garden is promoting peace among its neighbors as the endeavor involves Jewish families, Palestinians, Arabs, Christians, Muslims, and others. Through this initiative, we are not only praying for peace but sowing into and facilitating peaceful relations.

In a much broader sense, our entire My Olive Tree project is a fulfillment of Amos 9:11–15:

> "On that day I will raise up
> The tabernacle of David, which has fallen down,
> And repair its damages;
> I will raise up its ruins,
> And rebuild it as in the days of old;
> That they may possess the remnant of Edom,
> And all the Gentiles who are called by My name,"
> Says the LORD who does this thing.
> "Behold, the days are coming," says the LORD,
> "When the plowman shall overtake the reaper,
> And the treader of grapes him who sows seed;
> The mountains shall drip with sweet wine,
> And all the hills shall flow with it.
> I will bring back the captives of My people Israel;
> They shall build the waste cities and inhabit them;
> They shall plant vineyards and drink wine from them;
> They shall also make gardens and eat fruit from them.
> I will plant them in their land,
> And no longer shall they be pulled up
> From the land I have given them,"
> Says the LORD your God.

As a family and as an organization, we have taken these covenant promises quite literally, and we have managed to get others on board as well. When our Israeli manager, Sam, shared these Scriptures with an army base commander in the Negev Desert, the commander responded that after reading this he had no choice but to allow us to plant there because it was "God who instructed us" to "do this thing"—both the Jews and "all the Gentiles." (This outreach has become a physical demonstration of the importance of Jew and Gentile working together as "one new man.") The army base then released land and water to us so that we could plant olive trees on Israel Defense Force bases (IDF) in the Negev.

The base commander's partnership with our work was imperative, because the Israeli army controls the water in that region. But his cooperation is helping turn the desert green, and the legacy of My Olive Tree will be his as well.

One of the mysteries of legacy is understanding that lives speak louder and longer than words. Our children and our grand-children and those who come after us will remember more about how we lived than all the things we said. Our life example will outweigh the words we speak. Moreover, if how we live lines up with our words, then the wisdom we impart to others will have a better chance of being remembered.

Our legacy is our story, a parable of cultural principles that delivers a certain cause and effect. Every human being will leave a life legacy, a path, a story, some kind of impact. The mark we leave is either our earthly DNA or our changed spiritual DNA. We leave the fruit of the works of our flesh or the fruit of the works of the spirit, or a combination thereof.

You may not someday realize that you are Jewish, as I did, but when you were born again, you were grafted into a heritage that began with Adam and Eve, was consecrated by Abraham, Moses, David, and others in the Old Testament, and was fulfilled by the life, death, and resurrection of Yeshua. That whole rich spiritual heritage is now yours.

However, being grafted in, born again, and filled with the Holy Spirit does not ensure that your God-given purpose, your destiny, will be fulfilled. I am challenging you to return to the roots of biblical instruction, where you will find the keys of iden-tity, purpose, and power. When biblical instruction is applied, you will not find legalistic bondage but liberty that is practical and applicable today. That liberty will empower you to live and leave a legacy of your own.

Many years ago I witnessed a most profound testimony of allowing your life to develop into a legacy when we surrender to the authority of God. Making the choice to follow God's ways is not always easy, but it does leave a profound impact on future generations, as was demonstarated by Israel Meir Lau, the chief rabbi of Israel. At the time, I was interviewing him for a series we produced, *Men of Israel Today*, which featured quite a few distinguished government officials and some of Israel's top leadership. During our conversation at the Mount Zion Hotel in Jerusalem, Rabbi Lau shared his personal story.

All legacies come at a price, and for some the price is very high. The pain in Rabbi Lau's story was so palpable that I could barely keep my composure while the cameras rolled and the TV lights shone bright and hot. Christie sat off camera the whole time, silently weeping and overcome.

As a child, having lost both of his parents during the Holocaust, Lau was imprisoned at Buchenwald, one of the largest German concentration camps. It opened in 1937 in a wooded area in East Germany. The camp was liberated in 1945, at which time Rabbi Lau was a frightened seven-year-old boy. To evade the retreating Nazis, he hid himself in a pile of emaciated Jewish corpses, but his eyes moved back and forth, keeping a watch of his surroundings. A Jewish American soldier spotted the movement and lifted him out from among the dead.

The soldier wept at the sight of him. "How old are you, my child?" he asked in Yiddish.

Lau's remembered response has stuck with me to this day. "What difference does it make? I am older than you."

"Why do you think that you are older than me? I am a soldier—look at my uniform."

The seven-year-old Lau said, "Because you cry and you smile like a child. I stopped laughing years ago and even to cry? I do not cry anymore. So who is older?"

In Israel many years later, that "old" child had grown to understand the principle of traditions and heritage as well as the importance of national identity. In our interview I sensed there was something extraordinarily different about him compared to everyone else we spoke with for the series. In hindsight, I realize that it was in part because of his very deep connection with his own personal legacy and his grasp of the link between our choice and our destiny. When I asked him what the Holocaust taught him, he shared,

> It is only in our hands. Don't be fatalistic and say, "What can I do?" People who are fatalistic and meet each other in difficult times say, "What will be?" This is not the real question: "What will be?" The question has to be: "What shall we do?" not "What will be?" *"What will be?"* says "I have nothing to say" or "nothing to do." "What shall we do?" and "What shall be?" and "What shall *really* be?" That is the question. "What shall we do to leave a legacy, live a life of purpose, and create our destiny?"[2]

More recently, while in Atlanta for the opening of a synagogue, Rabbi Lau shared an interview with another Holocaust survivor, Ben Hiller. In the course of the interview, when Hiller shared both his pain over losing his family and his pride in his two sons, Rabbi Lau wisely pointed out,

> This is the *nachas* [joy or blessing, particularly in one's children]. This is also the greatest victory. You kept *Yiddishkeit*, Judaism. The Nazis' war wasn't only against Jews. It was also a war against Judaism. They destroyed 1,046 *shuls* [synagogues]

in one night on *Kristallnacht* [the "night of broken glass" when Nazis stormed the Jewish neighborhoods and smashed shop windows]. They didn't take the Jewish banks, clinics, stores—just synagogues. So when you survived and you built a nice family, it's a double victory, physically and spiritually.[3]

In Jewish tradition, you plant a vineyard for your children, and you plant an olive tree for your grandchildren. This tradition is implied by Proverbs 13:22:

> A good man leaves an inheritance to his children's children,
> But the wealth of the sinner is stored up for the righteous.

Rabbi Lau had a keen understanding of this principle of legacy and has kept his thousand-year lineage of thirty-eight generations of rabbis unbroken. His own son, David Baruch Lau, whom I have also had the honor and privilege to meet, has followed in his father's footsteps and is now the Ashkenazi chief rabbi of Israel.

Not all of us have the privilege of having our children and grandchildren follow so literally in our footsteps. But it is still our responsibility as parents, grandparents, and leaders to instill a sense of true legacy in those who come after us. Sadly, in western culture, legacy is too often seen simply as inheritance and is thought of mostly in terms of possessions—heirlooms, money, properties, vehicles, and so on. We have to train our minds to think of inheritance in a much broader sense.

Nachalah is the Hebrew word that most closely relates to what I mean by legacy; it means "inheritance, possession, property" but also relates to the idea of heritage and a portion or share.[4] We see this in the story of Jacob and Esau where Jacob laid claim to Esau's portion as the firstborn. Esau's stolen inheritance was about more than just possessions; it was also about standing and position.

When the Bible talks about leaving an inheritance to your children's children, it refers to much more than possessions. It is a matter of anointed instruction that becomes a biblical culture inside a family unit, part of the spiritual DNA that affects how your family interacts with the kingdom of God worldwide.

If you are a parent or a grandparent, it's your biblical responsibility to help your ceiling become your children's floor and your children's ceiling become your grandchildren's floor—building for them an inheritance of godly business, godly ministry initiatives, and godly relationships that help build Yeshua's kingdom here on earth, just as it is in heaven. And even if you don't have children, you still have a responsibility to the next generation.

The responsibility of dominion that God gave humanity can only be multiplied beyond us through the education of those who come after us. Christie and I long ago made the decision that we wanted the Landry family legacy to extend beyond the transfer of wealth. We believed it was our responsibility to equip our daughter, Megann, first and foremost for her calling in the kingdom and also to model for her a lifestyle of hard work, prayer and fasting, faithfulness in keeping the feasts of the Lord, diligence in tithing and offerings, and lived-out love of God and neighbor. We model to our children when the life that is portrayed and taught from the pulpit is the same as the life lived in the home. Today we are grateful to see the fruit of these efforts in the lives of Megann, currently the COO of Curt Landry Ministries and House of David, and Paul—and to know that they are passing on those lessons and modeling to Ariebella.

We are also observing similar outcomes with our spiritual children at House of David and hearing similar testimonies through Curt Landry Ministries' partners. Christie and I are so excited to witness an ongoing legacy of kingdom solutions in the face of a multitude of earthly problems. As powerful as discovering my biological heritage has been for me, I am being reminded that one doesn't need to be a parent to leave a powerful family legacy.

To keep our children and families (including our spiritual families) free from the enemy's corruption, we must raise them up in the fear and admonition of the Lord through love and respect, but they must also see that the instruction is working. Legacy is the fruit of working God's instruction and having it turn into a testimony of God's goodness that will last for generations to come.

The Jewish people are constantly reminded of their roots and their family legacy when they refer to the "God of Abraham, Isaac, and Jacob." This phrase itself ensures that they will never have another god. Their provision and their identity, purpose, and destiny all flow through this one source, so that Abraham's family legacy—which is our legacy as well—will continue. For God's promise applies to all of us who call Abraham Father and Yeshua Savior:

> And I will make your descendants multiply as the stars of heaven;
> I will give to your descendants all these lands; and in your seed
> all the nations of the earth shall be blessed. (Genesis 26:4)

As a pastor and a leader, I have spent years observing very successful people, and I have learned that those who are truly happy and energized have two things in common. First, they have a healthy respect for what we refer to as their calling, the purpose for which God created them. And second, they have invested time and energy discovering or uncovering their roots and heritage. They have taken time to understand their own spiritual DNA and how it applies to the bigger picture. Making peace with these two important elements of their God-given identity brings peace and purpose into their lives and paves the way for even further success.

In order to live well and leave a legacy, we must discipline ourselves and intentionally change our habits and patterns so that we create an atmosphere conducive to empowering that legacy. This requires a commitment to hard work and a certain "daily grind." Just as you must exercise and challenge your muscles if you want to grow stronger physically, you must repeatedly challenge yourself and practice your faith to build it up to accomplish bigger dreams.

As Rabbi Lau said, we must ask ourselves: *What shall we do?* We cannot operate from a victim mentality. We must make sure that our choices impact our destiny and our legacy.

In closing, I hope that this book will prepare a table for you in the presence of your enemies and that the Lord will anoint your head with the oil of your new identity in Him. My prayer for you and for all of us is that we would have an appreciation of God's mysteries and God's ways. May His instruction be as joy set before us so that we might labor together into the rest of the Lord and His biblical truth—*emunah*. May we experience the true joy and honor and wisdom that God shares as we come into agreement and alignment with His Word.

Praise the Lord that we all prophesy in part and look through a glass dimly (1 Corinthians 13:12)—because there is always more to learn and discover. May this small part of discovering and reclaiming your lost roots and forgotten heritage enable and assist you to live and leave a legacy as you uncover greater *shalom* in your Father God—the God of Abraham, Isaac, and Jacob to whom we have gained access through *Yeshua ben David, Yeshua ha Mashiach* (Yeshua son of David, Yeshua the Messiah).

For this reason I bow my knees to the Father of our Lord Jesus Christ, from whom the whole family in heaven and earth is named, that He would grant you, according to the riches of

His glory, to be strengthened with might through His Spirit in the inner man, that Christ may dwell in your hearts through faith; that you, being rooted and grounded in love, may be able to comprehend with all the saints what is the width and length and depth and height—to know the love of Christ which passes knowledge; that you may be filled with all the fullness of God.

Now to Him who is able to do exceedingly abundantly above all that we ask or think, according to the power that works in us, to Him be glory in the church by Christ Jesus to all generations, forever and ever. Amen. (Ephesians 3:14–21)

ACKNOWLEDGMENTS

THIS BOOK HAS BEEN A JOURNEY and in some ways represents the journey of a lifetime. It is truly more than my story; it is our story. A story made possible by many dedicated lives and hearts.

I could never curate a full list of the many people who ultimately were a part of *Reclaiming Our Forgotten Heritage* but I would like to acknowledge just a few.

House of David family, I love to worship and learn with you each week. You truly are the very best. Thank you for loving me.

Curt Landry Ministries and House of David staff, you are incredible gifts not only to me and to my family but to the kingdom. Thank you for co-laboring with us. Thank you for your hearts and unmatched dedication.

Tom and the Viral Solutions Team, you are excellent in everything you do for us and with us—we are grateful for your commitment. Thank you for growing with us.

Esther and The Fedd Agency, thank you for helping us on this incredible journey. There have been a lot of firsts!

Rick, thank you for helping us find the words and shape our story to be the best it could be.

Jeris, ever grateful for your heart, research, and insightful input.

John R., thank you for believing in us.

Webster and Janene and all the team at Thomas Nelson, thank you for the opportunity to share our story and taking the leap with us.

Thank you Pastor Tim and Sandy Alsbaugh for your true friendship, love, and dedication. Thank you for opening your home and your hearts to my family and helping us birth House of David. And to Brian who has gone ahead of us. The Alsbaugh family has been the truest of friends and family.

And to my wife, Christie, whose enduring love, support, prayers, and friendship not only made this book possible but made this journey possible. Thank you for your faith and sacrifice; *this is truly our story—thank you for living it with me.* I am so grateful you finally said yes! Oh, and thank you for always laughing at my jokes. Even when you aren't supposed to. I love you.

Megann, without you none of this would be possible. Your calling, devotion, dedication, and love has empowered your gifts to birth a ministry and calling not only in the United States but also in Israel. Your mom and I could not be more proud of or grateful for your hard work; thank you for sharing your gifts with us and the nations. Reclaiming *our* forgotten heritage is secure and could not be entrusted into better hands than yours, Megann Marcellino. Love, Dad.

Paul, many of the great exploits in Israel and in ministry would not have been possible without you and your service. Thank you for your vision, dedication, and perseverance.

Ariebella, thank you for your hope and unconditional love. Your calling and purpose make all of this legacy make sense.

Appendix

PRAYERS

A PRAYER AGAINST FALSE IDENTITY

Father God,

In the name of Yeshua, I repent and renounce any words that I have spoken over my life that have fed into the lie of a false identity. I ask You to forgive me for my sins of not believing that You have created me in Your image, for Your purpose, and with Your authority. Let the Holy Spirit come and baptize me with fire into the true purpose and identity of who I am in Yeshua, my Messiah. I welcome and receive all the gifts that God has blessed me with since conception, and I activate them and call on them to prosper now in Yeshua's name.

I acknowledge that I am a son/daughter of the seed of Abraham. I am grafted into the King of the universe by my salvation in Yeshua. He has made me His king and priest. He has empowered me by His Holy Spirit to take dominion on the earth as a king and in heaven as a priest. I am the head and not the tail. I am an ambassador empowered to reverse all curses and release blessings in their place. I am more than a conqueror through Yeshua, my Messiah.

Lord, I pray that You would heal my mind, will, and emotions from all past damage from false identity. I decree and declare that the devil is a liar and the father of all lies. I come out of agreement with all lies and word curses over my life, and I choose today to forgive all those who have spoken them over me. As the Scriptures tell us, "The thief does not come except to steal, and to kill, and to destroy. I have come that they may have life, and that they may have it more abundantly" (John 10:10).

I decree and declare that I am forgiven for ever blaming God the Father or Yeshua the Son for putting something on me or punishing me. I come out of agreement with that thought pattern, doctrine, and confession. I decree that God put on me His highest and best when He gave me His Son's blood to expunge and remove my sin. In Yeshua's name, I pray for the release of my true identity that is found in Christ alone and for all the provision, health, relationships, wisdom, knowledge, and understanding necessary for me to walk in my true identity.

I seal this prayer now in the name of Yeshua, amen.

A PRAYER FOR
STANDING IN FAITH

Father God,

Thank You for empowering me to stand in faith this day. I am grateful for Your guidance and Your loving care for me. I am truly honored to stand my watch over that with which You have entrusted me. I acknowledge that You paid a high price for my life and I appreciate Your gift of Yeshua that You freely gave to me for the removal and the expunging of my sin. I decree that the blood of Yeshua covers all areas of my life, and I thank You for the Lamb of God who takes away all my sin.

Abba Father, I cry out to You this day. I proclaim: I will take my place on Your wall. I am teachable. I am flexible. I will listen and receive correction because You correct those who You love, and You love me. I will be prepared by faith to receive my life's assignment. I will be prepared to see a new vision and to write it down by faith. I will be patient, and I will be humble as Your vision is revealed to me little by little. I freely humble myself under the hand of God, and I thank You in advance for calling me to Your good work.

I willingly surrender today, knowing that all things work together for the good of those who love You. I love You, Lord, and I know that You will do exceedingly abundantly above all that [I] ask or think, according to the power of the Holy Spirit within me.

Lord, today I come boldly into the courts of heaven, and I decree over my life now, according to Your eternal purposes that You accomplished in Christ Jesus my Lord in whom I have boldness and access with confidence through faith in Yeshua, that Yeshua is the Author and Finisher of my faith.

He is also the Author and Finisher of my life. I decree that I will trust in Him and trust that according to His Word I shall not be put to shame. I love you, Abba Father. In Yeshua's name and by the power of the Holy Spirit in me, I seal the workmanship that was prepared for me in my life today.

In Yeshua's name, amen.

PRAYERS FOR SHALOM IN MY LIFE

DAILY PRAYER FOR IDENTITY

Father God,

In the name of Yeshua, I believe and agree that I am a holy son [or daughter] of the King of the universe. I have been made to prosper. I have been made to multiply. I have been made to live in covenant agreement and reap covenant blessings from my God. According to Your Word, You

*have made me as king and priest, and You have empowered me by Your
Holy Spirit to take dominion on the earth as a king and in heaven as a
priest. I am the head and not the tail. I am an ambassador empowered
to reverse all curses and release blessings in their place. I receive this new
identity in You.*

In Yeshua's name, amen.

DAILY PRAYER FOR PURPOSE

Father God,

    *In the name of Yeshua I acknowledge that You have created me for
Your purpose. I dedicate my time, tasks, and activities for the equipping
and discipleship of all nations. I will do my work as unto the Lord. Let
my habits and patterns reflect that of a true disciple. I will teach my
family and friends to observe all things according to biblical instruction.
I will purpose to redeem that which has been lost in His kingdom and live
in alignment with God's love and instruction.*

    In Yeshua's name, amen.

DAILY PRAYER FOR DESTINY

Father God,

    *In Yeshua's name today I take authority over my destiny by disci-
plining myself to seek first God's kingdom and His instruction over the
world's ways. I take responsibility to receive all the benefits of operating
in God's economy. I agree that God will meet all my needs according to
His riches and glory through Yeshua our Messiah. I will remain sensitive
and generous to the Holy Spirit's promptings to be a part of the financial
assistance to help build His kingdom. I decree and declare that I cannot
out-give God and that I will be a cheerful giver.*

    *Lord, I thank You for an abundant destiny with no lack. I have
faith that as I do the small thing You will do the big thing. Lord, I ask*

for favor and grace in every daily task set before me. I receive Your grace, mercy, and shalom to be abundantly productive and to walk out my destiny, that I may prosper and live in health and peace.

In Yeshua's name, amen.

A PRAYER FOR MULTIPLICATION IN MY MISSION AND PURPOSE

Father God,

In the name of Yeshua, You have brought me to this place to deliver me from a mind-set of lack that is rooted in the spirit of poverty. I am convicted (not condemned) that I have filtered my expectations through lack and that this has affected the way I think about the generosity of God's provision and has robbed me of the fullness of what You have planned for my life.

I decree and come out of agreement with the spirit of poverty that has attached itself to my family and myself. I bind it and dismantle it, and I cast it into the lake of fire, where it cannot attach itself to me or to any of my descendants.

I speak a blessing of prosperity over my family for a thousand generations according to Your Word. We receive "exceedingly abundantly above all that we ask or think," as written in Ephesians 3:20.

Holy Spirit, come now and bless me with Your fire to burn out all the lying spirits that have created doubt and unbelief and have created false identities that do not belong to me. I am a new creation. All things have been made new.

May You, Holy Spirit, the power that works within us, finish the good work that was begun within me the day I came to Yeshua.

In Yeshua's mighty name, I seal it, amen.

NOTES

INTRODUCTION

1. How Jesus' name would have been pronounced by His parents and contemporaries.

CHAPTER 1: THE POWER OF HERITAGE

1. "The Declaration of Independence: The Want, Will, and Hopes of the People," USHistory.org, http://www.ushistory.org /declaration/document/ (accessed June 29, 2018).

2. Gabe Friedman, "10 Jews in Forbes Top 50 Billionaires," *Times of Israel*, March 3, 2015, https://www.timesofisrael.com/10-jews-in -forbes-top-50-billionaires/.

3. David Masci, "How Income Varies Among U.S. Religious Groups," Pew Research Center, October 11, 2016, http://www.pewresearch.org/fact-tank/2016/10/11 /how-income-varies-among-u-s-religious-groups/.

4. Daniel Kurt, "Are You in the Top One Percent of the World?" Investopedia, February 2, 2018, https://www.investopedia.com /articles/personal-finance/050615/are-you-top-one-percent-world.asp.

5. Barna Group, "America Divided on the Importance of Church," Research Releases in Culture and Media, Barna, March 24, 2014, https://www.barna.com/research/americans-divided-on-the -importance-of-church/#.VL09cYh0ycx.

6. Barna Group, "America Divided on the Importance of Church."
7. It should be noted that the scripture often refers to kings and priests, but these roles are not defined by the male gender; they are rather a spiritual call and authority for both sons and daughters.

CHAPTER 7: ACCIDENTALLY JEWISH

1. The term *Messianic* signifies Jews who have accepted Jesus as the Messiah but who retain their Jewish culture, customs, and traditions.
2. *Shabbat* is the Hebrew pronunciation of *Sabbath*. In Jewish communities the Sabbath begins at sundown on Friday and continues until sundown on Saturday, just as it did in Jesus' time.

CHAPTER 8: FINDING MY FATHER—AND MYSELF

1. Not her real name.

CHAPTER 10: THE GOD WHO KEEPS COVENANT

1. The Mosaic covenant is somewhat of an addendum to the Abrahamic, since it was made with the children of Abraham, Isaac, and Israel, and spelled out the blessings of Abraham bestowed on those who obeyed the law.

CHAPTER 11: THE CHURCH OF THE NEW TESTAMENT

1. Lois A. Tverberg, "God's Kind of Righteousness," EGRC.net, 2005, http://www.egrc.net/articles/Rock/HebrewWords2/God%27sRighteousness.html.

CHAPTER 12: OUR STOLEN HERITAGE

1. Maxwell Stamforth, trans., Andrew Louth, ed., *Early Christian Writings: The Apostolic Fathers* (New York: Penguin Classics, 1968), 73.
2. Justin Martyr, *Dialogue with Trypho*, trans. Marcus Dods and George Reith, rev. and ed. Kevin Knight, ch. 29, New Advent,

http://www.newadvent.org/fathers/01282.htm (accessed July 7, 2018).

3. St. Irenaeus, *Against Heresies*, trans. Alexander Roberts and William Rambaut, ed. Alexander Roberts, James Donaldson, and A. Cleveland Coxe, rev. and ed. Kevin Knight, book 3, chapter 22, New Advent, http://www.newadvent.org/fathers/0103321.htm (accessed July 8, 2018).

4. Earl Cox, "The True Face of Christendom," *Jerusalem Post*, February 7, 2017, https://www.jpost.com/Blogs /Israel-Uncensored/The-True-Face-of-Christendom-480779.

5. Earl Cox, "The True Face of Christendom."

6. Origen of Alexandria, *Contra Celsum*, trans. Frederick Crombie, rev. and ed. Kevin Knight, book 4, ch. 22, New Advent, http:// www.newadvent.org/fathers/0416.htm (accessed July 8, 2018).

7. Augustine, *City of God*, 18.26, in Paula Fredricksen, *Augustine and the Jews: A Christian Defense of Jews and Judaism* (New Haven, CT: Yale University Press, 2010), xii.

8. Heinrich Graetz, *History of the Jews*, vol. 2 (Philadelphia: Jewish Publication Society of America, 1893), 563–564.

9. "Letter from the Synod in Nicaea to the Egyptians," trans. and ed. Norman P. Tanner, "First Council of Nicaea—325 AD," *Papal Encyclicals Online*, http://www.papalencyclicals.net/councils /ecum01.htm (accessed July 7, 2018).

10. "Antisemitism in History: From the Early Church to 1400," *Holocaust Encyclopedia*, United States Holocaust Memorial Museum, https://www.ushmm.org/wlc/en/article. php?ModuleId=10007170# (accessed July 7, 2018).

11. Judah Gribetz et al., *The Timetables of Jewish History: A Chronology of the Most Important People and Events in Jewish History* (New York: Touchstone, 1994).

12. Yerachmiel Ben Avraham, *All in the Name of Jesus: The Murder of Millions* (Aurora, CO: Wavecloud, 2016), 162; and "The History of the Jewish People: 1742," JewishHistory.org, http://www .jewishhistory.org.il/history.php (accessed July 7, 2018).

13. "The Holocaust: An Introductory History," Jewish Virtual
    Library, www.jewishvirtuallibrary.org/an-introductory-history-of-
    the-holocaust (accessed July 7, 2018).
14. "This Day in History: September 5, 1972: Massacre Begins at
    Munich Olympics," History.com, https://www.history.com/this
    -day-in-history/massacre-begins-at-munich-olympics (accessed
    July 7, 2018).
15. "ADL Data Shows Anti-Semitic Incidents Continue to Surge in
    2017 Compared to 2016," ADL, November 2, 2017, https://www.
    adl.org/news/press-releases/adl-data-shows-anti-semitic-incidents
    -continue-surge-in-2017-compared-to-2016.
16. "ADL Data Shows Anti-Semitic Incidents Continue to Surge in
    2017 Compared to 2016."
17. "ADL Data Shows Anti-Semitic Incidents Continue to Surge in
    2017 Compared to 2016."
18. Derek Prince, *The Destiny of Israel and the Church: Understanding
    the Middle East Through Biblical Prophecy* (New Kensington, PA:
    Whitaker House, 2016), 15, 123.

CHAPTER 13: ONE NEW MAN

1. It should be noted that this leadership team did not create the
   alignment intentionally. It was truly the sovereign hand of God
   assembling apostolic leadership from the First Nations (Native
   Americans), firstborn Jews, and firstfruit Gentiles (Christians;
   Gentiles are considered the firstfruits of the Jewish olive tree; that
   is, they are the firstfruits of Jesus' ministry and the expansion of
   the gospel outside the walls of Judaism).
2. The Gregorian calendar is the one we use today. It was introduced
   by Pope Gregory XIII in 1582. It was a slight modification of the
   Julian calendar.
3. The *seder* is the traditional feast held on the first night of Passover.
   It takes place around the world on the evening of the fifteenth
   day of the Jewish month of Nisan and includes reading Scripture,
   telling stories, drinking wine, eating special foods, singing, and

other activities. Each element of the meal has a special meaning
and reflects what was eaten at the first Passover in Egypt,
described in Exodus 12.
4. A feast schedule is available at www.CurtLandry.com
/FeastTime.

CHAPTER 14: FAITH

1. "530. emunah," Bible Hub, http://biblehub.com/hebrew/530.htm
(accessed July 8, 2018).
2. "539. aman," Bible Hub, http://biblehub.com/hebrew/539.htm
(accessed July 8, 2018).
3. W. E. Vine, Merrill F. Unger, and William White Jr., *Vine's
Complete Expository Dictionary of Old and New Testament Words*
(Nashville: Thomas Nelson, 1996), s.v. "faith."
4. Tzvi Freeman, "What Is Emunah? Beyond Belief," Chabad.org,
http://www.chabad.org/library/article_cdo/aid/1398519/jewish
/Emunah.htm (accessed June 8, 2018).
5. Tzvi Freeman, "What Is Emunah? Beyond Belief."
6. Tzvi Freeman, "What Is Emunah? Beyond Belief."
7. "3320. yatsab," Bible Hub, http://biblehub.com/hebrew/7235.htm
(accessed July 8, 2018).

CHAPTER 15: SHALOM

1. W. E. Vine, Merrill F. Unger, and William White Jr., *Vine's
Complete Expository Dictionary of Old and New Testament Words*
(Nashville: Thomas Nelson, 1996), s.v. "peace."
2. W. E. Vine, et al, *Vine's Complete Expository Dictionary of Old and
New Testament Words*.
3. "Hebrew Names of God: The Holy One Revealed in the
Tanakh," Hebrew for Christians, http://www.hebrew4christians.
com/Names_of_G-d/Holy_One/holy_one.html (accessed
July 8, 2018).
4. "571. emeth," Bible Hub, http://biblehub.com/hebrew/571.htm
(accessed July 8, 2018).

CHAPTER 16: MULTIPLICATION

1. "7235. rabah," Bible Hub, http://biblehub.com/hebrew/7235.htm (accessed July 8, 2018).
2. Daniel Lapin, *Thou Shalt Prosper: Ten Commandments for Making Money* (Hoboken, NJ: John Wiley & Sons, Inc., 2010), 153–154.
3. *Strong's Concordance*, s.v. "memshalah," https://www. blueletterbible.org/lang/lexicon/lexicon.cfm?t=kjv&strongs =h4475 (accessed July 8, 2018).

CHAPTER 17: LEAVING A LEGACY THAT EMPOWERS

1. You can learn more about our efforts at www.MyOliveTree.com.
2. Interview with Israel Meir Lau for *Men of Israel Today*, http://www .aish.com/jw/s/Rabbi-Israel-Meir-Laus-Revenge.html.
3. Ronda Robison, "Rabbi Israel Meir Lau's Revenge," Aish.com, July 15, 2017, http://www.aish.com/jw/s/Rabbi-Israel-Meir-Laus -Revenge.html.
4. "5159. nachalah," Bible Hub, http://biblehub.com/hebrew/5159. htm (accessed July 8, 2018).

ABOUT THE AUTHOR

CURT AND HIS WIFE, CHRISTIE, travel extensively, preaching and teaching about the Jewish roots of the Christian faith. Together, their passion is to empower families to live and leave kingdom legacies and understand their own spiritual heritage. Curt and Christie are also actively involved in raising support for Israel within the evangelical community and have participated with the delivery of millions of dollars in aid to Israel and the nations. Curt Landry is the founder of Curt Landry Ministries, House of David Ministries, and My Olive Tree.